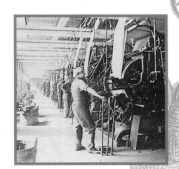

The World of Wooden Bobbins

Drawing Box

RESEARCHER: Pauline Fawcett

DESIGNER: David Harban

EDITOR: Graham Fellowes

ACKNOWLEDGEMENTS.

The following people have been generous with their own time and research material.

Ann and Dirk Poole

David Harris

RESEARCH CONSULTANTS AND STUDY CENTERS

Marian Hall and the research staff at the Museum of American Textile History, N. Andover/Lowell, Massachusetts.U.S.A.

Lloyd Hutchins, Jr., Barre, Vermont, U.S.A.

Bill Johnson and the research staff at the Slater Mill, Pawtucket, Massachusetts. U.S.A.

Lowell Historical Park, Lowell, Massachusetts, U.S.A.

Merrimack Valley Textile Museum, U.S.A.

Marion Pomerance (editorial assistance), Wellesley, Massachusetts, U.S.A.

Mike Millward, Blackburn Textile Museum, Blackburn, Lancashire, England.

John Dixon of John Dixon and Sons Ltd., bobbin manufacturerers 1795 – 1983

Louanne Collins, Curator, The Heritage Centre and Paradise Silk Museum, Macclesfield, Cheshire, England.

Brian Butler and staff of Joseph Horsfall & Co, Worsted Spinning Mill, Halifax, Yorkshire, England.

Alison Vincent, Marketing Manager and Vincent Newton of the Textile Dept., Manchester Museum of Science and Technology, Lancashire, England.

The Archive Department of Oldham Museum, Oldham, Lancashire, England.

Roger Pilkington of Pilkington's Shuttles, Belgrave Works, Heywood, Lancashire, England.

Maurice Dunnett, Archivist, Saddlesworth Museum.

Sue Latimer, Curator of Saddlesworth Museum, Uppermill, Nr Oldham, Greater Manchester, England.

The Stott Park Bobbin Mill, Ulverston, Cumbria, England.

Styal Mill Museum, Styal, Cheshire, England.

ISBN 0-9646720-0-6

PUBLISHED BY: The Discovery Collection
P.O Box 10, 401-403 Kennedy Boulevard, Somerdale, New Jersey 08083 U.S.A.

Copyright © 1995 The Discovery Collection
Printed in England by KNP Group Ltd.

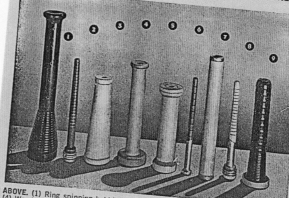

LOWELL SHUTTLE COMPANY

MANUFACTURERS OF
BOBBINS AND SHUTTLES FOR COTTON, **WOOLEN, WORSTED, RAYON, SILK AND CARPET MILLS**

Established 1896

15 TANNER STREET, LOWELL, MASS.
Telephone: GLenview 2-1151

Incorporated 1914

OVER 50 YEARS UNDER SAME MANAGEMENT

LOWELL BOBBINS

Maple, birch or beech wood, as required. For spinning, twisting or weaving of cotton, wool, worsted, rayon or silk. Wood is well seasoned and kiln dried (when necessary). Finished with oil, lacquer, shellac or baked-on enamel, as required. Carefully inspected and only perfect products passed for shipment.

ABOVE. (1) Ring spinning bobbin. (2) Automatic loom bobbin. (3) Winder cone. (4) Worsted twister bobbin. (5) Winder tube. (6) Bobbin for non-automatic loom with electric feeler motion. (7) Warp spinning tube. (8) Automatic loom bobbin for electric feeler motion. (9) Worsted spinning bobbin.

BELOW. (1) Shuttle for carpet loom. (2) Shuttle for automatic wool or worsted loom. (3) Shuttle for plain worsted loom. (4) Shuttle for automatic cotton loom (equipped with brass threader). (5) Shuttle for automatic cotton loom (equipped with cast iron threader). (6) Shuttle for silk or rayon loom (equipped with Paterson tension and fibre covered on one side).

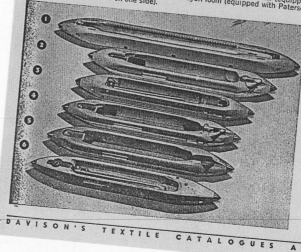

LOWELL SHUTTLES

Widely recognized for their quality for over half a century, Dogwood or persimmon, fibre covered or plain, as specified, for weaving of cotton (including duck), wool, worsted, silk, rayon, paper and carpets. Fibre covering protects delicate yarns and is applied to STAY. Wood is thoroughly seasoned, kiln dried and finished to specifications.

DAVISON'S TEXTILE CATALOGUES AND BUYERS' GUIDE

CONTENTS

Appreciating Our Old Bobbins

The mid 1900s, with its relentless technical advances, was a sad time for wooden bobbins. With the introduction of open-ended spinning and plastic bobbins, traditional spinning and wooden bobbins quickly became a thing of the past.

Unfortunately, wooden bobbins had become far too commonplace to be valued, and whole mill stocks were destroyed. Bobbins were not even valued as firewood, as their high oil content created hazardous fires that burned out of control. So, millions and millions of wooden bobbins were thrown away or burned in landfills. While no one can be entirely sure, it has been estimated that three quarters of the wooden bobbins made, many of which were still in use in the 'fifties, have been destroyed.

Fortunately, collectors have begun to appreciate bobbins as objects of character and interest from a time of true craftsmanship, and are busy harvesting these relics from the few remaining mills as they either modernize or close down.

Wooden bobbins and shuttles are becoming increasingly valuable as they become increasingly rare.

Now is a good time to start collecting. Wooden bobbins are still affordable and obtainable; they offer a fascinating hobby and a good investment !

LIFE BEFORE BOBBINS

For millions of years animal skins were man's only protection from the cold. It was later in human development that people turned to wool for warmth and, in fact, wove with plant fibers long before weaving with wool.

To make the wool fibers stick together, they were twisted and pulled. The production of a continuous piece of thread is known as spinning, but fibers have first to be cleaned and carded, and arranged so that they are all pointing in the same direction.

In ancient times spinning was achieved by using a spindle and a distaff. The cleaned and loosely wound fiber, or roving, was wound round the distaff which was held under the arm. The roving was then gently pulled and twisted and attached to a tapered stick; the spindle. The pulling and twisting of the roving caused the spindle to turn or spin, producing a long unbroken thread of wool.

Then followed weaving. The warp threads were attached lengthwise to the loom and the weft thread, attached to a shuttle, ran between the warps. Weaving in this way was extremely time consuming. The production of enough cloth for a humble shawl might have taken as long as a week.

Spinning with the use of a distaff. The yarn is spun by twisting the spindle at the spinner's feet.

Egyptian spinners using two spindles to produce yarn from flax. This picture is from the walls of a tomb at Beni Hasan in Egypt, approximately 1,900 BC.

ANCIENT DAYS

Some ancient civilization produced fabric well before the time of Christ. The Chinese had a thriving silk industry more than two thousand years B.C. Fine quality cotton was produced in Egypt for nearly three thousand years B.C., and the classical Greeks had their own highly skilled spinners and weavers.

The Romans, at the height of their Empire, set up the first recorded spinning and weaving factories. They established Britain's first textile factories which were built during the Roman occupation, some 1,500 years before the Industrial Revolution. The first was a military weaving establishment, 'gynaeceum', set up by the Emperor Diocletian in Winchester. A dye works was set up at Silchester, and cloth finishing shops called Fullonicae, were set up in major towns. Wool was so highly prized that it was often used in place of money.

At the fall of the Roman Empire in the 5th century, the legions left Britain, taking their advanced production methods with them. The British tribes returned to their traditional methods of spinning and weaving. Cloth production was to remain a cottage industry until the invention of the steam engine brought about the Industrial Revolution.

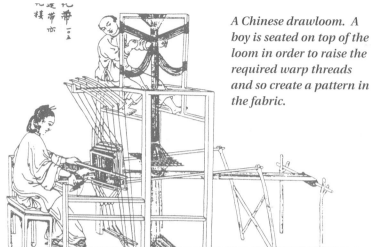

A Chinese drawloom. A boy is seated on top of the loom in order to raise the required warp threads and so create a pattern in the fabric.

THE SPINNING WHEEL was a major innovation around 1100 AD. This was the limit of technological advance for another 300 years, when the BOBBIN AND FLYER WHEEL appeared. This allowed continuous spinning of the yarn.

English woolen goods were the most highly regarded textiles in the world until the arrival of the cotton trade in the 1800s. When skilled workers from northern Europe sought refuge in Britain to avoid religious persecution, they introduced new fabrics and weaving methods such as worsted stuffs and cotton mix cloths. Broadlooms came into greater use at this time, producing wider fabrics, requiring two weavers to throw the shuttle across the loom.

MECHANIZATION APPROACHING

In the 1700s, with improvements in farming machinery, selective breeding, crop rotation and more efficient land usage, many small farmers became redundant, and moved to the growing towns to find employment. Most had some weaving and spinning skills and readily found employment in the growing textile industry. Some merchants and clothiers set up small 'loomshops', in an attempt to centralize production. Spinners and weavers were often now wholly employed away from their homes. These 18th century loomshops were the forerunners of bigger things by far.

Yorkshire and Lancashire in the north of England are still associated with wool and cotton manufacturing respectively.

Many loomshops are still standing today in England.

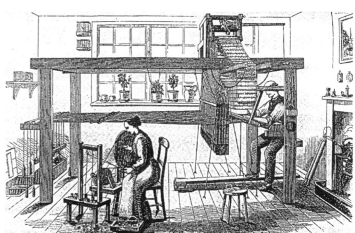

Jacquard loom in a weaver's garret

1 *ROVING bobbin 10" x 2".* **2** *DRAWING bobbin 16" x 9" plywood flanges c.1890.* **3** *9½" finisher barrel/drawing roll.* **4** *8" x 2" TWISTER, copper head, rare half-binding on base.* **5** *6" TWISTER.*
6 *5½" CAP SPINNER ⌣ unusual slim base band.* **7** *5" CAP TWISTER, worsted, ⌣ copper/brass shields.* **8** *4" x 3" silk bobbin.* **9** *CAP SPINNER, ⌣ brass head.*
10 *Warp SPINNING bobbin, acorn head, made for export to S. America, China, Japan. (Rabbeth spinning; cotton).* **11** *CONE ROVER 11" x 5" with speeder hole/dog-holed washer.*
12 *6" TWISTER or SPINNING bobbin, ⌣ single ended.* **13** *9" heavy laquered TWISTER, brass shields.* **14** *#5 butt QUILL with optical tape and oblong hole.*
15 *8" Northrop-type PIRN (shuttle bobbin) metal sensor, single saw slot.* **16** *Abbott 7" winder CONE.*

17 *5" CAP SPINNER, unusual narrow metal band.* **18** *5" CAP SPINNER* ◯. **19** *Two-part base, 6½" TWISTER,* ◯, *worsted.* **20** *Warp creel bobbin: 5" x 3".* **21** *Spinning FRAME bobbin; wool, 12" x 2½" x 2".* **22** *Spinning FRAME bobbin, wool: 12" x 2½" x 1½".* **23** *5" x 2½" Silk or Rayon spool. (Robson's, Huddersfield).* **24** *Spinning FRAME bobbin, 12", worsted yarn mill.* **25** *Frame KING or JACK bobbin knitting yarn 12" x 2½".* **26** *Magnum TWISTER: 12" x 2½" x 2".* **27** *Heavy yarn/shield-cord TWISTER. 10" x 5" x 3" Arundel Couthard machine or Platts. Tufnell head, one-piece metal base.* **28** *6" x 4" rope-making spool.* **29** *10" x 4½" BRAIDER bobbin.* **30** *5½" single-ended CAP SPINNER/TWISTER* ◯.

THE GROWTH OF THE COTTON INDUSTRY IN ENGLAND

Lancashire, England, provided the perfect environment for the production of cotton textiles. The moist air helped the fibers to hold together, reducing the strain imposed on them by the new machines. Land prices were low and there was an abundant supply of water and coal. Liverpool was an ideally situated port and Manchester an ideal mercantile center.

Crank Mill, built in 1790 at Morley, was one of the first steam-driven mills in Yorkshire

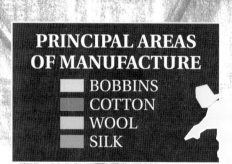

PRINCIPAL AREAS OF MANUFACTURE

- BOBBINS
- COTTON
- WOOL
- SILK

SCOTLAND

Aberdeen

Glasgow • Edinburgh

• Newcastle

Cumberland
Westmorland

• Middlesborough

Yorkshire

Lancashire   Bradford   Hull
                        Leeds
Liverpool Manchester
         Macclesfield   • Lincoln
Cheshire
                  • Nottingham

                                    Norwich •
Shrewsbury   ENGLAND

      Birmingham
WALES   Cambridge
Worcester • Stratford upon Avon   Ipswich

    Gloucester
              Oxford
                        London
  Bristol
                                    Canterbury
            Southampton

Exeter •   Dorchester

Plymouth •

By 1790 spinning factories were spreading across England. Until then, factories relied on fast flowing streams to drive the machinery. But with James Watt's invention of The Rotative Steam Engine in 1781, mills could rely on steam power. The steam engine gradually replaced the waterwheel as the industry's main power source. The resulting increase in spun yarn meant there was a shortage of weavers, who became very highly paid in consequence.

STYAL MILL

At Styal Mill in Cheshire, the mill owner, Samuel Greg, provided what in those days, were excellent working conditions. He provided good housing and leisure facilities for his workers. A non-conformist, he ran his factory on enlightened humanitarian lines. He even ensured that medical and dental care were available to all his workers.

Styal Mill, set in a beautiful wooded valley, is now run by the National Trust of Great Britain as a fully working museum.

COTTON

Britain's industrial supremacy in the 1800s was dependent upon raw cotton which had to be imported. Around the time that supplies from the West Indies were proving inadequate, the cotton fields of the American South were developing. American planters were progressive and, by consistently improving productivity were able, for many years, to bring about a steady reduction in prices. The invention of Eli Whitney's cotton gin added further impetus to a fast-growing industry.

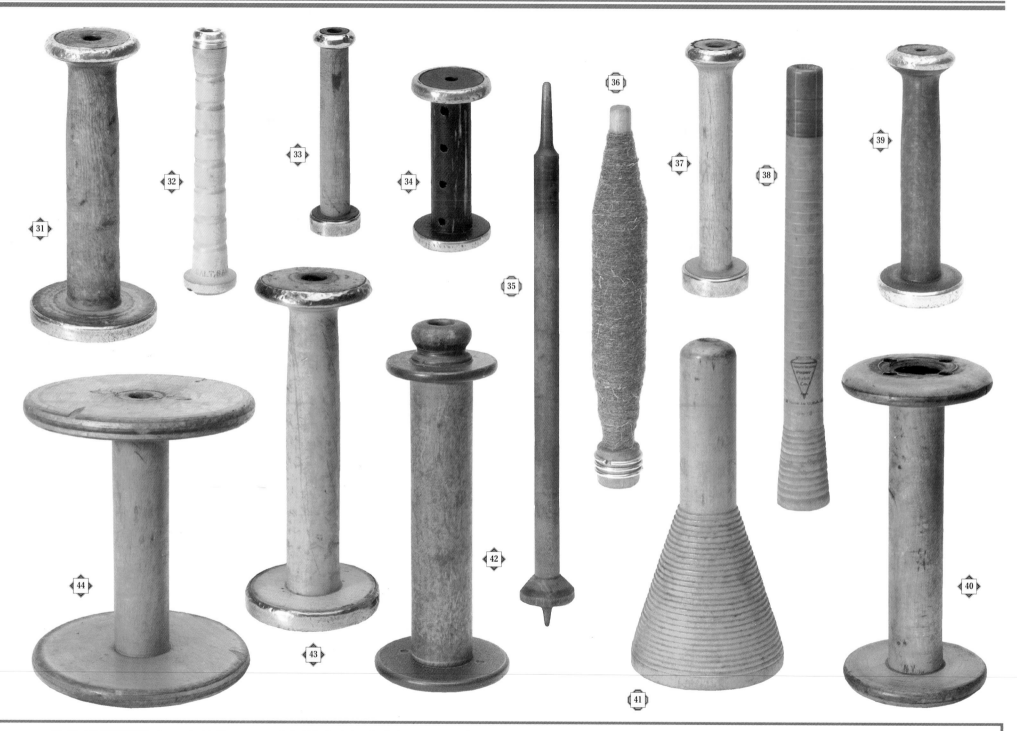

31 9" x 3½" TWISTER, ◯ wool. **32** 8" custom-made bobbin for Salts of Saltaire. Spinning, when full, went direct to weaving department. **33** 5" rare old brass head CAPSPINNER, wholly shielded base. **34** 5" steamer bobbin ◯ copper, black protective laquer. **35** Cotton slubber/spinner. **36** QUILL loaded with yarn. C&K or Draper loom quill. **37** 6½" TWISTER. **38** 12" paper tube. Cotton. **39** 7" x 2" brass and copper TWISTER c. 1880. **40** 9" x 4" CONE ROVER with unusual drive fitting, (see page 55). **41** Frame KING bobbin, 9" x 4" x 1½" for sewing yarns. **42** 9½" x 3½" x 3" Leesona #514 TWISTER spool with doffing knob. **43** 9" x 2½" TWISTER, worsted. **44** Warper or creel bobbin 7" x 5½".

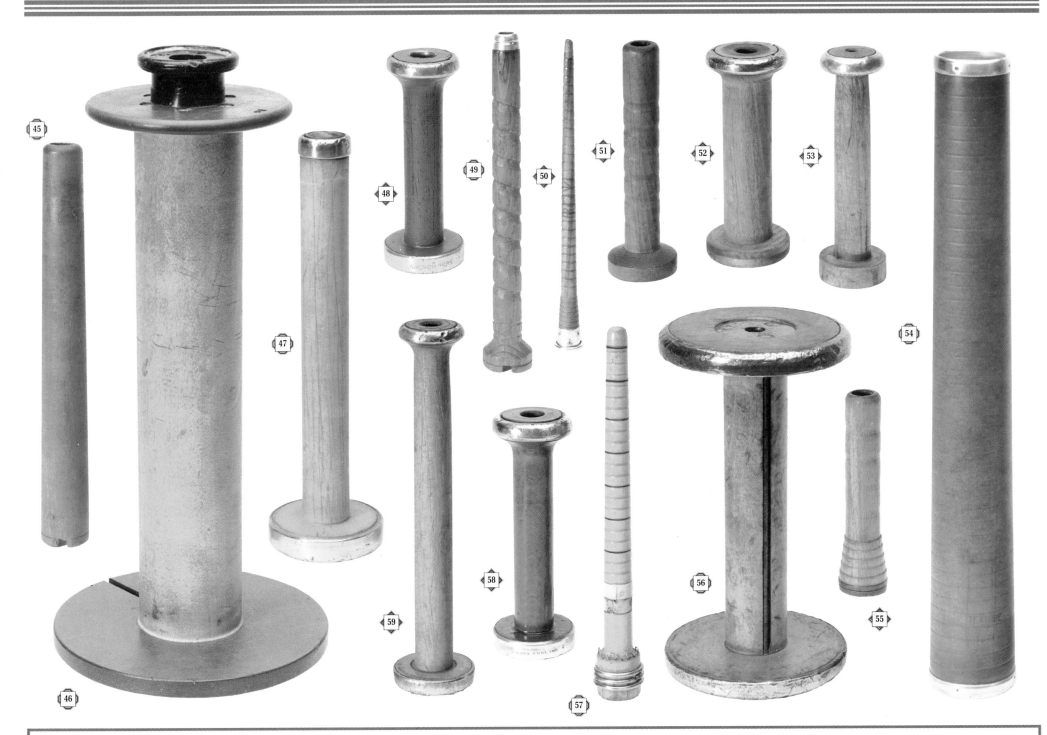

45 *Spinning FRAME bobbin for small ring frame, 9" possibly custom-made for Pendleton Woolen Mill.* **46** *Heavy yarn TWISTER with doffing knob: 16" x 7½" x 5½".* **47** *Large package TWISTER: 11" x 3".*
48 *CAP TWISTER 5½" with blue protective coating, brass core, copper shields.* **49** *Custom made shuttle QUILL, 8" for a blanket loom.* **50** *8" compressed paper QUILL.* **51** *6" CAP-TWISTER, single ended.* **52** *CAP TWISTER.*
53 *Copper ended 5" CAP TWISTER.* **54** *Fine yarn, paper tube 15" x 2½" x 1½".* **55** *Sally TWISTING bobbin, 5" for cotton.* **56** *11" x 6" shield cord TWISTER for Whitin twisting frame, wired for extra strength.*
57 *Leesona 9" unifil auto QUILL with optical tape. Refilled on loom itself; 14 per machine.* **58** *6" Cap TWISTER made by Dixons, brass shields, protective laquer.* **59** *Boyd spinning bobbin 9".*

THE SLATER MILL

English immigrant Samuel Slater and Providence merchants William Almy and Smith Brown built the Slater Mill in Pawtucket, Rhode Island in 1793, for the production of machine-spun cotton. As the first factory in America to successfully produce yarn with water-powered carding and spinning frames, the Slater Mill is considered the birthplace of America's Industrial Revolution.

The mill today is open to the public and beautifully maintained as a fascinating exhibition.

The American and British textile industries harnessed the energy from rivers to drive the shafts, gears and belts of the large water wheels. This use of water wheels was, in the United States, second only to those used for milling grain.

Riverside mills would quickly dominate the industry and bring undreamed of efficiency and profit.

In the early 1800s, America experienced a shift towards the use of cotton. Until now, yarn had been made from wool and flax, as sheep flourished on the pastures of New England and flax was easy to grow.

Cotton required by the mills of North America and England created a new class of businessmen and merchants. Some bought and organized the transport of the raw cotton to the mills, while others specialized in the retailing and shipping of the finished product.

THE INDUSTRIAL REVOLUTION AND SOCIAL CONDITIONS

Were all the mills dark and satanic?

Any account of textile history would be incomplete without pointing out that working conditions during the Industrial Revolution were often very grim. Fortunately, there are surprising examples of paternalistic mill owners of exceptional vision and humanity.

The success of many English businessmen impressed American merchants. Many considered manufacturing cloth in the United States rather than relying on English imports, although they were often deterred by reports of degraded living and working conditions for what was perceived as a developing British underclass. With many lessons to be learned from England, The American Industrial Revolution was notable for its greater efficiency and productivity, and for its much improved working conditions.

The mills could be suffocating in summer and freezing in the winter months. Rules were many and harsh.

The factory system introduced long working hours and exploitation of child labor in dreadful working conditions. The independent handloom workers had to work even harder for lower wages in the face of this competition. Children were often required to work at machines fourteen hours a day. Accidents were many and the consequences were dreadful. They were beaten to keep them awake, poorly fed and badly clothed.

Adults and children suffered from industrial diseases; tuberculosis, lung problems caused by prolonged inhalation of dusty cotton fibers and certain cancers, especially of the mouth, caused by sucking the thread through the eye of the shuttle, known as 'KISSING THE SHUTTLE'.

THE GREAT TEXTILE MILLS

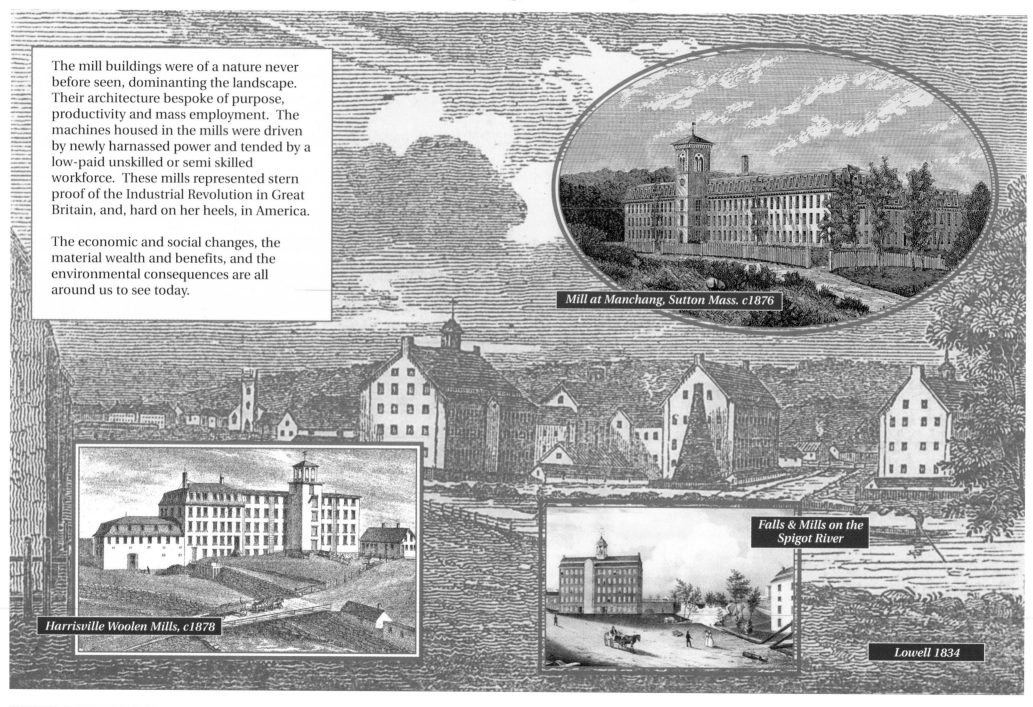

The mill buildings were of a nature never before seen, dominanting the landscape. Their architecture bespoke of purpose, productivity and mass employment. The machines housed in the mills were driven by newly harnassed power and tended by a low-paid unskilled or semi skilled workforce. These mills represented stern proof of the Industrial Revolution in Great Britain, and, hard on her heels, in America.

The economic and social changes, the material wealth and benefits, and the environmental consequences are all around us to see today.

Mill at Manchang, Sutton Mass. c1876

Harrisville Woolen Mills, c1878

Falls & Mills on the Spigot River

Lowell 1834

SALTAIRE
TITUS SALT 1803-1876

Salt came to Bradford in 1822 where his father set up as a wool merchant. In 1825 he entered the business but left after four years to start on his own as a worsted stuff manufacturer. Within only fifteen years he had made his fortune, largely because of his introduction of alpaca and other unusual fibers into worsted production.

By 1850 Salt was probably the richest man in Bradford, certainly the foremost employer and an established political figure in the town. He had five mills to his name, and strong commercial links with the European and American markets. It was around this time that he conceived the idea of Saltaire, a model industrial town dedicated not only to the production of the finest textiles in the world but also to the people, the ordinary working people who made it possible.

Salt set his mind to leaving Bradford in whose sky was hung a constant pall of yellow smoke and in whose streets could be seen the worst extremes of poverty and human degradation to be found in Britain. He chose the picturesque Aire Valley to build a mill that could straddle the river, canal and rail. A colossus of a mill filled with the latest innovations of construction and equipment, pleasing to the eye, and in efficiency, years ahead of its time.

When the mill was complete the town of Saltaire was built to house the working population in attractive Italianesque cottages. Then came a hospital, a congregational church and Methodist chapel, an institute, almshouses, public baths and washhouses. Finally a landscaped park in which the population of some 4000 could take the air that Sir Titus had pledged to protect.

A leader in industrialism, and a founder of paternalism, Sir Titus Salt had surely set an example for the world to follow.

Power loom c1820

60 *5" CAP SPINNER.* **61** *5" CAP SPINNER brass base.* **62** *7" x 2" TWISTER, ◇ worsted.* **63** *Heavy TWISTER 8" coned head.* **64** *5" CAP TWISTER.* **65** *4¹/₂" CAP TWISTER.* **66** *Cotton 16" ROVING bobbin.*
67 *14" x 5" TWISTING bobbin for rayon/cotton with doffing knob: Scragg or Lesona machine.* **68** *7" x 2¹/₂" flyer TWISTER: jute or mixed fiber, ◇ Machie machine.*
69 *8" x 3¹/₂" x 2" perforated steamer/TWISTER, ◇ copper and brass.* **70** *10" x 3¹/₂" heavy TWISTER ◇ Prince Smith, Stell machine for wool or worsted.*
71 *9" x 4" SPINNING bobbin for Mackie Jute or man-made fibers: rounded Tufnell on Bakelite.* **72** *8" x 2" TWISTER; copper, for fine yarns, suiting, worsted.* **73** *TWISTER, 10¹/₂" x 5" x 3¹/₂" for cotton.*

74 *Cotton warp bobbin 4¹/₂".* **75** *TWISTER* ⬭ *6¹/₂".* **76** *9" ring TWISTER* ⬭. **77** *Fiber quill, 8¹/₂" unidentified.* **78** *SPINNING bobbin, small ring, 8" king bobbin.* **79** *Late 1800s twister 7" x 2".*
80 *7¹/₂" cone head heavy TWISTER for worsted.* **81** *Shield cord bobbin 12" x 6¹/₂" for Rayon.* **82** *Haskell Dawes 7" x 6" rope making spool.* **83** *4" silk spool.* **84** *5" CAP SPINNER brass head.* **85** *5" CAP SPINNER.*
86 *Ring spinner 9".* **87** *FRAME bobbin 12" x 2¹/₂" worsted.*

Changing Fortunes

It was inevitable that the trade in Britain, which depended entirely upon imported raw materials, would sooner or later be hostage to events. The American Civil War (1861-64) was a prime example. The cotton famine brought on by the war was a damaging setback.

By the 1860s, other countries were already setting up their own cotton industries. Lancashire, England, had little to fear from Europe, but when cotton-growing and low-wage countries also became manufacturers, markets began to disappear. India was quick to develop her own textile industry and Brazil and Japan followed. By 1880 half the world's cotton consumption was in these new areas. In 1933 Japan introduced twenty-four hour working and became the largest exporter of cotton goods in the world.

For decades the British were the primary inventors of labor-saving machinery and theirs was the most advanced industry in the world, turning out high quality fabrics such as corduroy, velveteen, broadcloth, silk, satinette and fustian.

The British protected their position with a ban on the export of textile machines. This was eventually lifted in 1843 when Britain was the largest exporter of textiles to Europe and North America; a position which had required great secrecy in technical developments. Now she was to lose control of the world textile market.

Victims of the cotton famine as a result of the American Civil War

THE DECLINE OF THE COTTON INDUSTRY IN GREAT BRITAIN AND THE UNITED STATES

By 1803 cotton had overtaken wool as Britain's leading export; a position maintained until 1938 when precision machinery moved into first place. Sales of cotton yarn and goods accounted for over half of Britain's overseas earnings in 1830. By the First World War it had fallen to one quarter.

There was a short-lived revival of fortunes after 1918. Since then there has been a dramatic decline. In 1958 the British Government passed the Cotton Industry Act which compensated employers for scrapping old machinery. More than 12,000,000 spindles and 105,000 machines were scrapped. The dawn of artificial fiber brought more problems for a market under attack from cheap imports and more mills were forced to close. By 1980 the Lancashire cotton industry was history, and this sad situation was reflected in the United States.

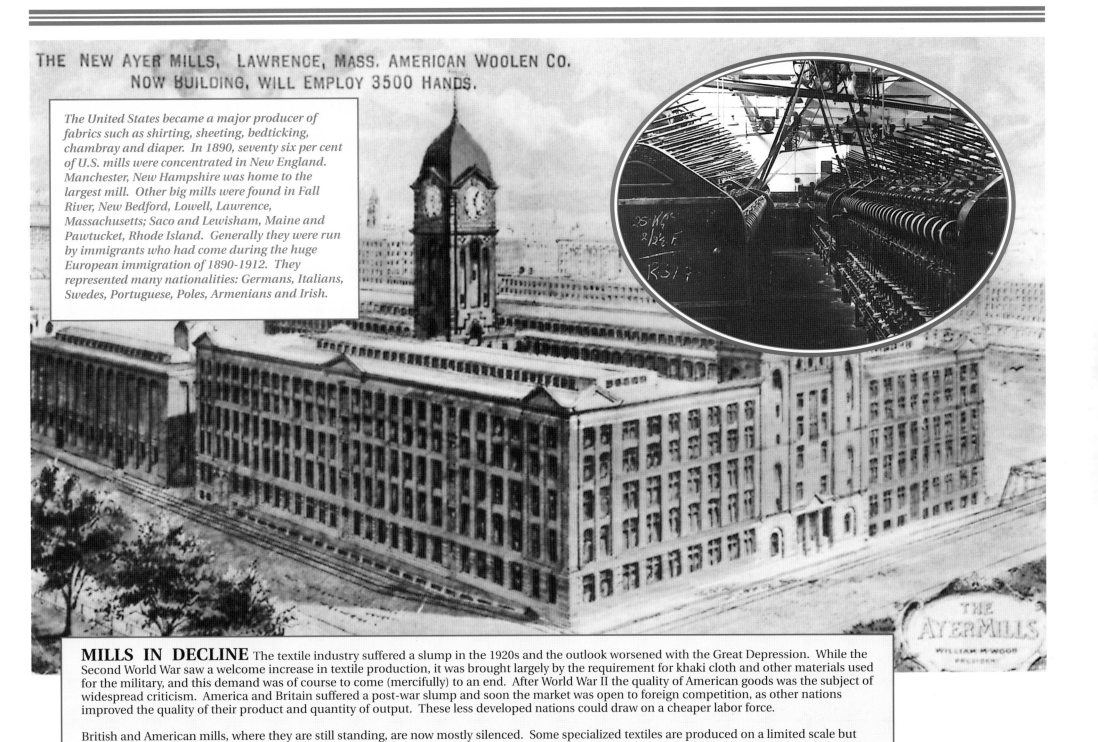

THE NEW AYER MILLS, LAWRENCE, MASS. AMERICAN WOOLEN CO.
NOW BUILDING, WILL EMPLOY 3500 HANDS.

The United States became a major producer of fabrics such as shirting, sheeting, bedticking, chambray and diaper. In 1890, seventy six per cent of U.S. mills were concentrated in New England. Manchester, New Hampshire was home to the largest mill. Other big mills were found in Fall River, New Bedford, Lowell, Lawrence, Massachusetts; Saco and Lewisham, Maine and Pawtucket, Rhode Island. Generally they were run by immigrants who had come during the huge European immigration of 1890-1912. They represented many nationalities: Germans, Italians, Swedes, Portuguese, Poles, Armenians and Irish.

THE AYER MILLS
WILLIAM M. WOOD
PRESIDENT

MILLS IN DECLINE The textile industry suffered a slump in the 1920s and the outlook worsened with the Great Depression. While the Second World War saw a welcome increase in textile production, it was brought largely by the requirement for khaki cloth and other materials used for the military, and this demand was of course to come (mercifully) to an end. After World War II the quality of American goods was the subject of widespread criticism. America and Britain suffered a post-war slump and soon the market was open to foreign competition, as other nations improved the quality of their product and quantity of output. These less developed nations could draw on a cheaper labor force.

British and American mills, where they are still standing, are now mostly silenced. Some specialized textiles are produced on a limited scale but many mills have been torn down or have been renovated for other purposes. In the course of this steep downward decline, over some 30 years, it is an unhappy fact that many interesting artifacts which had been in service for well over a century were sent to landfills.

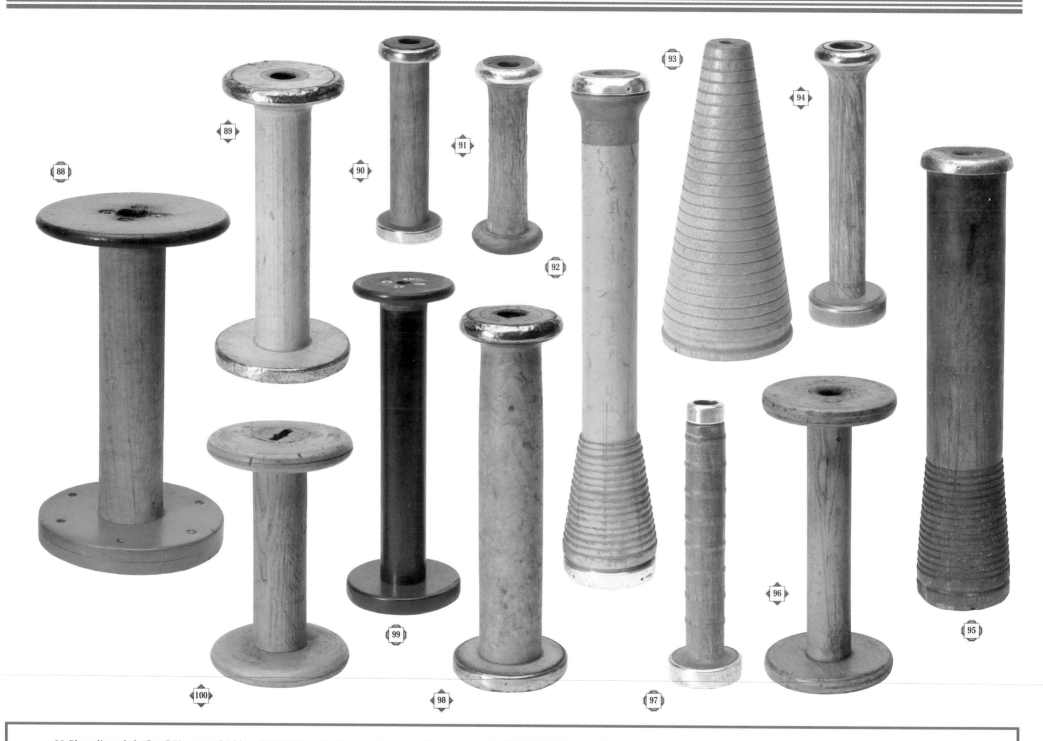

88 *Phenolic ended, 9" x 5" Firestone shield cord TWISTER.* **89** *8" twister. Prince Smith machine.* **90** *5" CAP SPINNER.* **91** *5" CAP TWISTER, brass,* ◯ *worsted.* **92** *13½" x 2½" FRAME bobbin. Woolen carpet.*
93 *Universal in-house winder CONE 7" x 3½".* **94** *7" TWISTER.* **95** *13½" FRAME bobbin, woolen carpet.* **96** *8" x 3" ROVER/FINISHER.* **97** *8" mule SPINNING bobbin with ridges.* **98** *10"x 3" heavy TWISTER.*
99 *Leesona 512 TWISTER spool 9" x 3" x 2½" phenolic ends.* **100** *6" x 3½" FINISHER bobbin. Single saw slot both ends.*

101 *4" silk spool .* **102** *Worsted 6" single ended* ⬭ *CAP TWISTER.* **103** *4½" x 2½" brass ends. Unidentified.* **104** *4" x 2" silk or rayon spool.* **105** *6" CAP TWISTER.* **106** *7" universal Abbott winder in-house CONE.*
107 *Cotton TWISTER, 9" x 3" Arundel or Platts machine.* **108** *7" x 3½" ROVING/FINISHING.* **109** *10" x 3" laquered TWISTER, Wilson Bros.* **110** *10" x 1" unidentified FRAME bobbin.*
111 *10" compressed paper QUILL, brass end.* **112** *10" x 3½" TWISTER.* **113** *9" x 3" cotton TWISTING. Arundel or Platts machine, bobbin by Wilsons.* **114** *BRAIDER bobbin. 7½" x 3"*
115 *9" x 4" shield cord TWISTER spool, phenolic ends.*

WHAT IS A BOBBIN?

A heap of thread is unmanageable and a ball is not much better. A bobbin is the answer, revolving on a driven spindle to collect the developing thread. Different stages require different bobbins; hence bobbins became known by the process for which they are intended – spinning bobbins, twisting bobbins, drawing bobbins, roving bobbins, finishing bobbins etc.

Some machines have hundreds of spindles in operation at the same time and on each one is a bobbin either releasing or collecting thread. Many mills had their own machine shops and their own favorite shape of bobbin. This accounts for the many and varied shapes of the older bobbins in the hands of collectors.

THE WOODEN BOBBIN IN SEMI-RETIREMENT

Modern economics do not favor wooden bobbins. A large degree of handwork is involved to make them and this has become expensive. Furthermore, they are not always efficient when used on the newer high-speed machinery. The introduction of man-made fibers also caused problems. The acrylic fiber had a tendency to stick to the wood. Plastic bobbins and cones, or those made of compressed paper or resinous fiber mix, were found to be more practical, and less expensive. Some mills, by virtue of a niche market, still employ the old machines and techniques, and it is still possible to have custom-bobbins and shuttles supplied. (See acknowledgements) Many Third World countries are also still producing goods with the use of wooden bobbins.

BOBBIN MANUFACTURE

In England, many of the early bobbin mills were situated in the Lake District. There was an abundant supply of water from the rivers and streams to supply water power to drive the machinery. Wood could be harvested from the forest-covered hills and valleys. Young trees were "coppiced" to achieve the right diameter. They were cut back to their base from which would grow several long poles instead of a single trunk. Birch and ash were the trees most commonly coppiced, but sycamore, alder, hazelwood and (imported) hickory were also used.

The poles would be cut and carted to the bobbin mills, more than sixty in the lakeland area. They would be stripped of their bark, often by young children. The poles were then cut into two main working sizes. The lower and thicker part was called the 'blocking' wood. This was cut up into 'cakes', and holes were punched out by a blocking saw. The thinner part of the poles were cut into lengths of different diameter to produce bobbins. The bobbin blanks were then bored through and cut into rough bobbin shapes.

The thicker wood was blocked on the blocking saw after being cut into 'cakes' of the required length. The blocking was done with a tubular saw and a 'parrot-nose' bit, punched out, 'roughed' and 'bored'. The wood then had to be dried and turned on a finishing lathe.

116 9" x 2¹⁄₂" x 2" novelty yarn TWISTER, brass. **117** 17" x 9" x 7" Arundel Couthard machine. Wool TWISTER. **118** Cotton TWISTER, 9" x 2" copper top. **119** 11" copper cotton SPINNING bobbin.
120 12" x 2" large package TWISTER. **121** 5¹⁄₂" single ended CAP TWISTER. ◯ Worsted. **122** 9" x 2¹⁄₂" TWISTER, copper top. **123** 5¹⁄₂" CAP TWISTER, by Dixons. **124** 5" CAP SPINNER ◯. **125** 5" CAP TWISTER copper top.
126 7" CHEESE core winder. **127** 10" x 5" TWISTER for heavy coarse yarn or shield cord. **128** 6" CAP TWISTER. **129** 7" TWISTER, worsted ◯. **130** 8" x 2¹⁄₂" brass and copper TWISTER, ◯ with protective laquer.

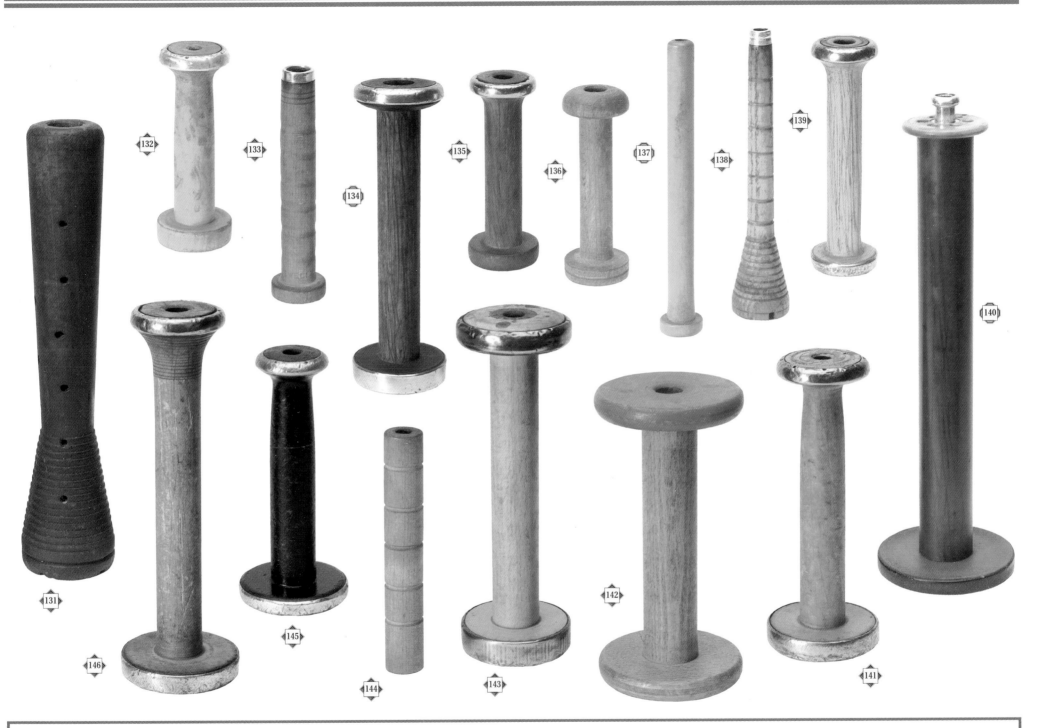

131 *12" FRAME bobbin. Spinning. Paper-maker's felt mill. Reverse taper.* **132** *5" CAP TWISTER, worsted, brass top.* **133** *5½" SPINNING tube.* **134** *8" x 2½" novelty yarn, TWISTER, brass ended.* **135** *5" CAP SPINNER* ⬭.
136 *5" CAP SPINNER,* ⬭ **137** *7" cotton slubber or SPINNING bobbin.* **138** *8½" Velox ring spinning PIRN.* **139** *6" CAP TWISTER* ⬭. **140** *16" x 4½" x 2½" rayon down TWISTER spool.* **141** *8" x 3" TWISTER* ⬭ *wool.*
142 *8" x 4" ROVING/reducing bobbin. Wool.* **143** *9" x 3" TWISTER/preparation bobbin, nylon or cotton rayon.* **144** *7" DRAWING roller or winding spool for weft cotton.*
145 *7" x 3½" TWISTER, brass and copper* ⬭ *heavy laquered for wet doubling or steaming.* **146** *10" x 3" cotton TWISTER, copper bottom, pegged base with speeder hole and dog-holed washer.*

Boring – The bobbin blanks were bored through using bench-mounted drills, producing a crude bobbin.

Roughing – The roughing lathe cut the wood to the approximate length, shape and diameter requested by the customer. This produced the two flanges and barrel of the bobbin.

Drying – When first cut, the wood was wet with sap. Before the bobbin could be finished it had to be completely dried in a drying room at the mill.

Finishing – Before the finishing process could be carried out the bobbin first had to be 'rinced' or 'reemered'. This involved the central hole being made larger and cleaned out. This was done using manual drills which produced a cleaner finish. After being reemered they were turned on finishing lathes and shaped with tools into the style and pattern demanded.

Polishing – This was done by placing the bobbins in a revolving polishing barrel, which contained a lump of paraffin wax. Half an hour of tumbling would produce a shiny protective surface on the bobbin, giving it the appearance of being varnished. Sometimes, on request of the individual mill owners, bobbins were dyed before polishing took place. The colors helped to identify a particular machine and sometimes related to the color of yarn. After being polished they were bagged for delivery.

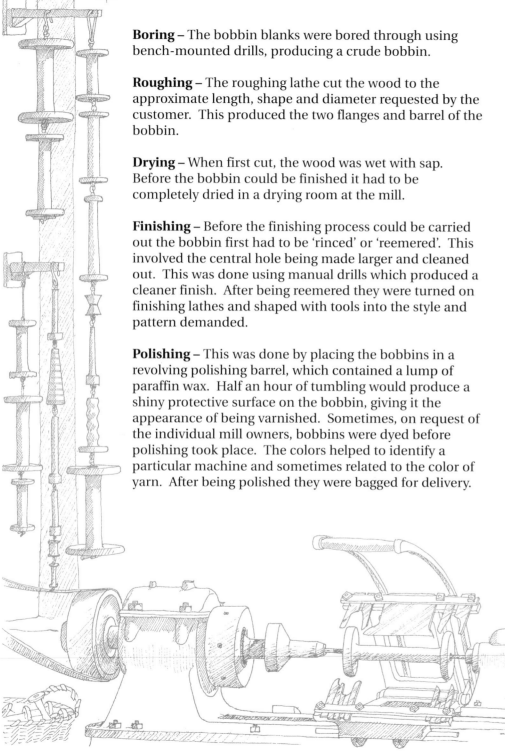

TOOLS USED IN THE FINISHING PROCESS

A **sliper** is a wide flat knife which determined the length and diameter of the barrel of a bobbin.

End tools were used to accurately cut the outside surfaces of the bobbin flanges.

Rounders shaped the top of the flanges.

Gougers cut the ends of the bobbins ready for the end tools to do their work.

Toppers prepared the flanges to be finished by the rounders.

Nickers cleaned out the inside edges of the flanges.

Bevellers produced an angled inside surface to the flange when required.

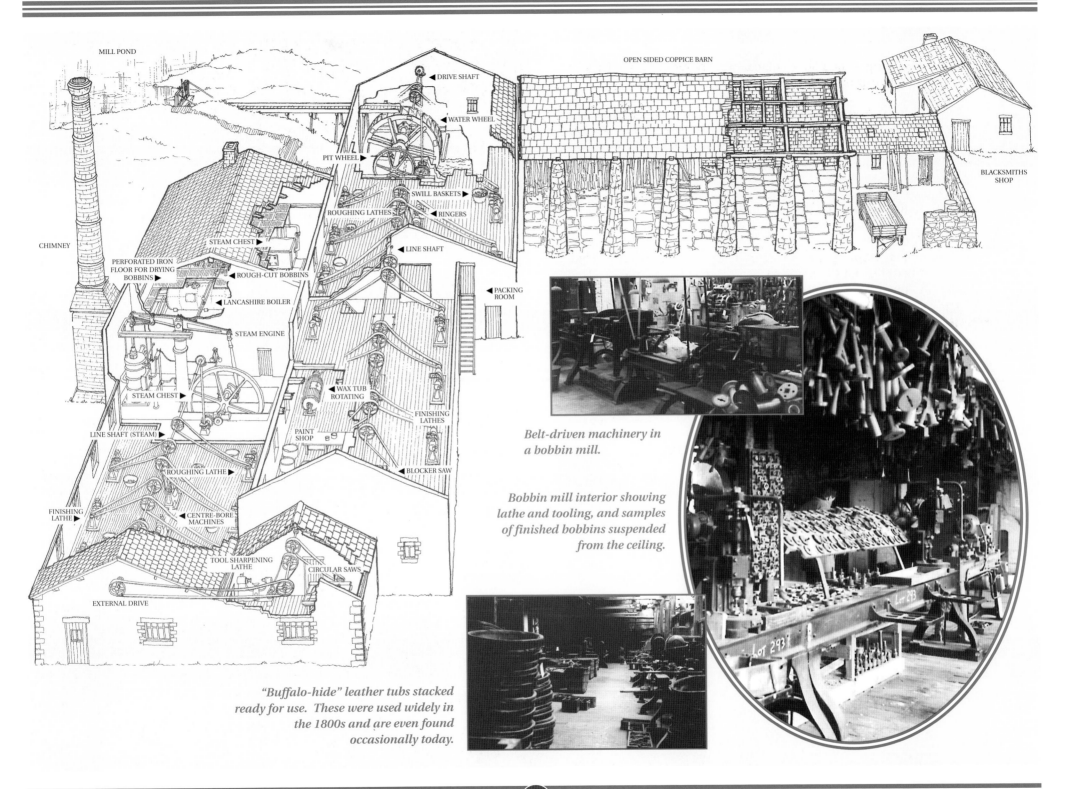

MILL POND

DRIVE SHAFT

WATER WHEEL

OPEN SIDED COPPICE BARN

PIT WHEEL

BLACKSMITHS SHOP

SWILL BASKETS

ROUGHING LATHES

RINGERS

STEAM CHEST

LINE SHAFT

CHIMNEY

PERFORATED IRON FLOOR FOR DRYING BOBBINS

ROUGH-CUT BOBBINS

PACKING ROOM

LANCASHIRE BOILER

STEAM ENGINE

WAX TUB ROTATING

STEAM CHEST

FINISHING LATHES

PAINT SHOP

LINE SHAFT (STEAM)

BLOCKER SAW

ROUGHING LATHE

FINISHING LATHE

CENTRE-BORE MACHINES

TOOL SHARPENING LATHE

CIRCULAR SAWS

EXTERNAL DRIVE

Belt-driven machinery in a bobbin mill.

Bobbin mill interior showing lathe and tooling, and samples of finished bobbins suspended from the ceiling.

"Buffalo-hide" leather tubs stacked ready for use. These were used widely in the 1800s and are even found occasionally today.

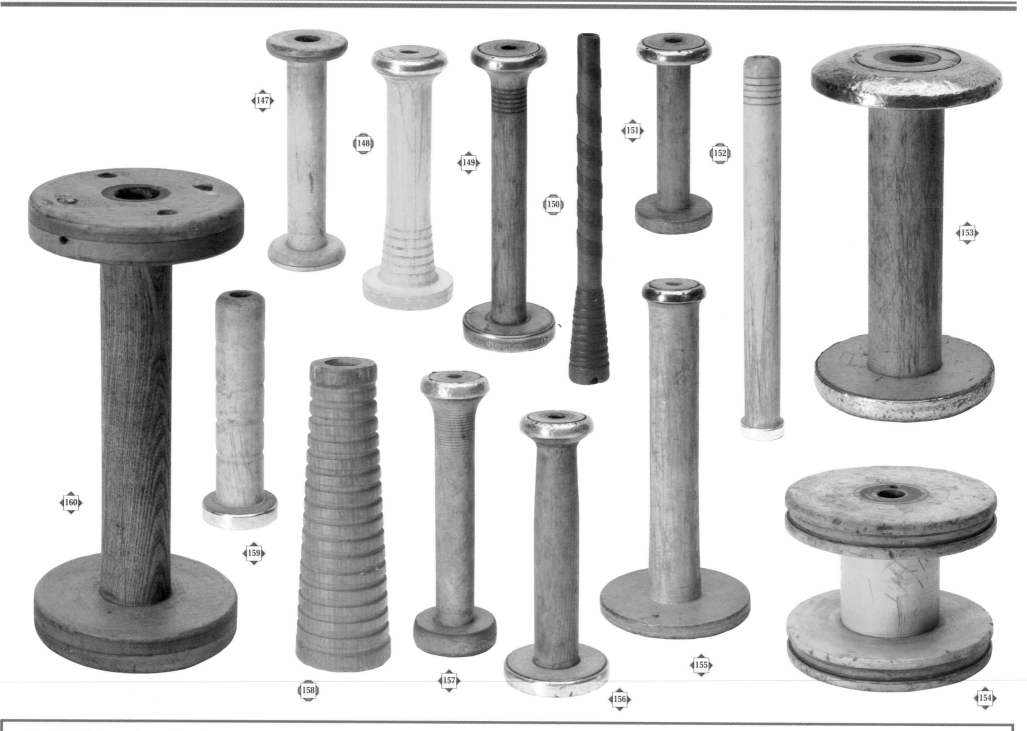

147 6" TWISTER, worsted. 148 6" x 2¹/₂" SPINNING bobbin. 149 8" x 3¹/₂" TWISTER, worsted, fine yarns. 150 8" spindle compressed paper, unidentified. 151 5" Cap TWISTER. 152 9" reverse taper, SPINNING bobbin.
153 9" x 5" ROVING bobbin, specialised construction, unidentified. 154 4" x 5" belt driven spool. Selvedge bobbin which runs within the loom. 155 9" x 4" unidentified.
156 7" x 3" brass ended ⬡ TWISTER for worsted. 157 7" copper head TWISTER. Arundel machine. 158 7" Abbott winder CONE.
159 6" heavy TWISTER, ⬡ worsted. 160 12" x 6" Prince Smith Stell machine ROVING bobbin with lead weights built in for accurate weighing of full package.

161 *FRAME bobbin for wool.*   **162** *7" x 2" fine yarn TWISTER, heavy laquered.*   **163** *6" x 3½" warp creel bobbin.*   **164** *13" paper tube, wool.*   **165** *5½" CAP TWISTER.*   **166** *7 x 3½" ROVING/reducing bobbin.*
167 *9" x 5" ROVING bobbin by Dixons.*   **168** *6" x 3" woolen yarn TWISTING spool.*   **169** *10" cap shuttle bobbin or QUILL. Metal alloy.*   **170** *8" mule SPINNING bobbin.*   **171** *10" x 2" x 1" brass ended worsted SPINNING bobbin.*
172 *7" x 3" wet TWISTER, cotton or asbestos, heatproof and waterproof laquer.*   **173** *7" x 4" reducer or FINISHER bobbin.*

THE ENGLISH LAKE DISTRICT supplied mills in Lancashire, Yorkshire, Ireland, Scotland and the United States with bobbins until the late 1800s. The arrival of steam power meant that bobbins could be produced anywhere. In the United States, production of bobbins was increasing, so further reducing the dependency on Britain.

The older (and now highly collectible) bobbins were turned from a kiln-dried blank of rock maple. The center was bored and often a brass bushing was inserted, improving the efficiency and life of the bobbin. The ends, or flanges, made out of cabinet-grade birch, were threaded and screwed on, and frequently laminated and glued. Some bobbin ends were drilled for hardwood locking pegs. This was an additional strengthener for the solid or plywood flanges. The spool had then to be turned and polished on a lathe before being coated with several layers of varnish. In many cases, protective metal bands were added at this stage and a hardened steel drive plate installed.

Until the mid-1800s bobbins were made in separate pieces. The pieces comprised the barrel of the bobbin and one or two flanges. In the early days, children glued end pieces (flanges) onto the central wooden cylinder (barrel). These bobbins can still sometimes be found. They are usually in excess of 150 years old. Later, new machinery pioneered by two inventors, Braithwaite and Fell, enabled some bobbins to be produced in one piece.

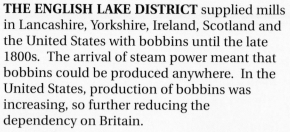

Ring Doubler showing some of the complexities of assembly: threaded ends, skew dowels and laminations.

STANDARDIZATION WAS NEEDED

in the early 1800s as the United States developed the 'American' style of manufacture. This was largely attributable to Eli Whitney and others, who pursued the production of interchangeable pieces using jigs and patterns. By the 1900s the production of textile machines was in the hands of a few major manufacturers and bobbins had to be interchangeable and standardized in order to prove efficient. Such standardized techniques were maintained in the U.S. right into the mid-1900s.

Warp and filling ring spinning frame.

TEXTILE WORLD

COTTON MACHINERY

REVOLVING FLAT CARDS With New Doffer Slow Motion, Etc.
DRAWING FRAMES
With Electric Stop Motion.
SELF ACTING MULES and TWINERS
For Coarse, Medium and Fine Counts.
Spindles, Flyers, Card Clothing and Other Textile
Sundries.
SLUBBING, INTERMEDIATE & ROVING FRAMES.

Tweedales & Smalley, Castleton, Eng.
Taylor, Lang & Co., Stalybridge, Eng.
William Ryder, Bolton, Eng.

H. C. McKerrow & Co.

Sole Agents in United States and Canada.
Worthington Bldg., 31 State St., BOSTON, MASS.

Glen Bobbin Co.

DEMAND FOR BOBBINS IN THE UNITED STATES

Samuel Slater in Rhode Island required large numbers of identical bobbins for the spinning frames. Because of this, small water-powered bobbin and shuttle shops were a common sight in many towns and villages of New England.

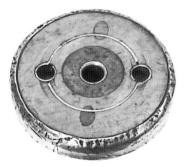

In order to protect the flanges, metal shields were added. In the damp atmosphere of the mills the tin rusted and discolored the yarn. Copper and brass were introduced, and used for over a century. Zinc plated steel and steel alloys followed in the early 1900s so that now copper and brass bound bobbins are increasingly difficult to find and should be especially cherished.

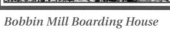

Bobbin Mill Boarding House

The American method of production was in principle the same as the British. Bobbins were of rock maple, birch, dogwood, apple, boxwood, hickory and occasionally walnut or cherry. Each set of bobbins for a particular machine had to be identical in weight. Small lead weights inserted in the flanges of the bobbins were used for balance, but flush to avoid the snagging of the yarn as it was spun onto them.

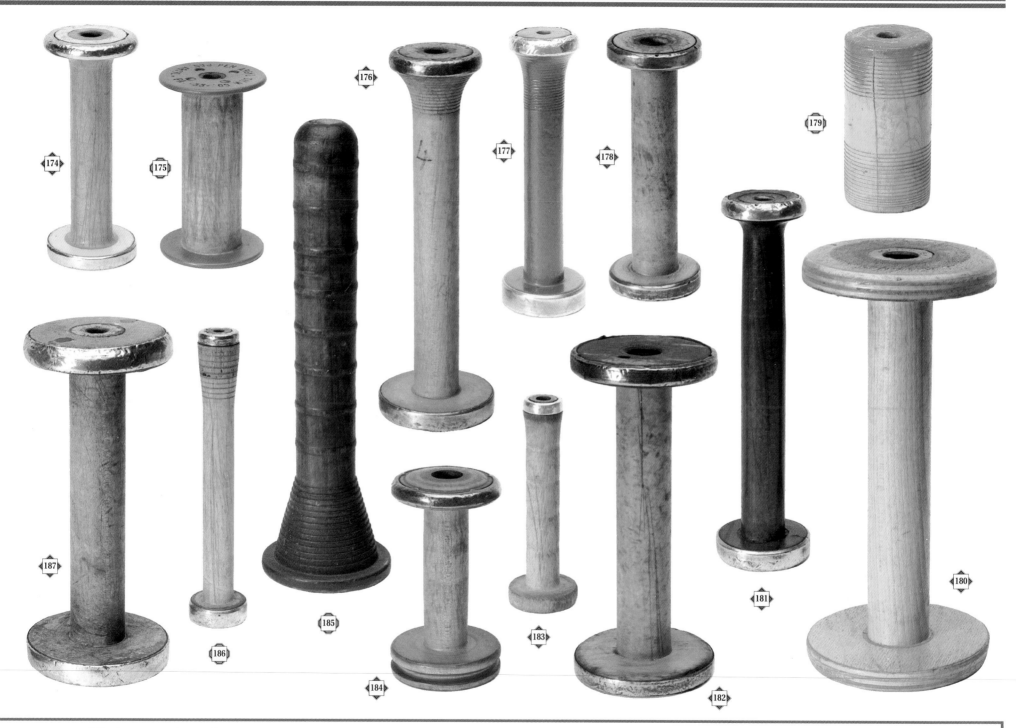

174 6" TWISTER, worsted. **175** 4" x 2" phenolic ended throwing-mill spool. **176** 10" x 3" x 2¹/₂" Boyd TWISTER, pegged base, speeder hole, dog-holed washer, wool/worsted or man-made mixtures.
177 7" TWISTER, copper head, protected against wet twisting with heavy green finish. **178** 7" x 2¹/₂" TWISTER ◇. **179** 4" x 2" Cotton CHEESE core, yarn storage. **180** 11" x 5" CONE ROVING bobbin.
181 10" TWISTER, heavy laquered, copper ended, brass bore. **182** 9" x 4" FINISHER bobbin. Arundel or Platts machine. **183** 5" TWISTER, single cap. Cotton. **184** Belt driven 5¹/₂" x 3" unidentified.
185 12" x 3¹/₂" x 1¹/₂" spinning FRAME bobbin for worsted yarn. **186** 8" cotton DOUBLING bobbin. **187** 9" x 4" brass ended, TWISTING, cotton or man-made fibers. Bobbin from Cromers Mill.

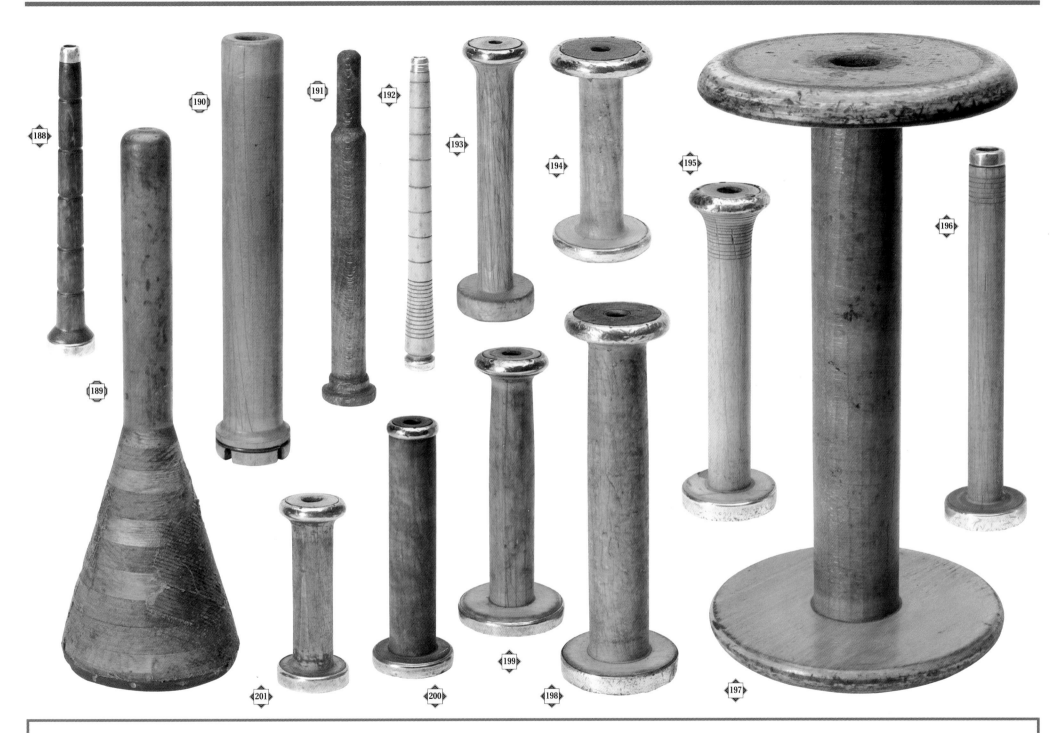

188 8" QUILL or pirn, ◯ brass tipped.   **189** 17" x 6" x 2" giant KING bobbin used in papermaker's felt mill.   **190** 12¹/₂" cottton ROVING bobbin.   **191** 9¹/₂" spindle, unidentified.   **192** 8" QUILL, copper tipped.
193 7" TWISTER, from Josiah Lumbs Mill.   **194** 5¹/₂" x 2¹/₂" SPINNING bobbin.   **195** 10" cotton SPINNING bobbin, brass shields.   **196** 9" TWISTING bobbin brass shields.   **197** 16" x 8" DRAWING bobbin, ply ends.
198 10" TWISTER, brass.   **199** 7" TWISTER ◯ late 1800's.   **200** 7" TWISTER bobbin.   **201** 5" CAP SPINNER, worsted ◯.

DIFFERENT BOBBINS AT WORK

Larger bobbins carried the loose coils of roving while small bobbins and pirns stored the finished, finely spun yarn which was ready for weaving.

The older draw-box bobbins and roving or finishing bobbins had a single hole in the center of each flange. Many of these are more than 100 years old.

When the machinery became more sophisticated in the mid-19th century, some bobbins had metal bushings inserted in the flange holes. This extended the life of the bobbin by preventing wear.

Some bobbins were designed with slots, peg holes, drive slots and drive plates fitted to one of the flanges. There were corresponding protrusions from the machine to grip or drive the bobbin.

One of the largest bobbins seen is the 16" x 7" or even 16" x 9" roving bobbin from the English worsted system. These were nicknamed 'buffets', an old local word for a small stool. In the process, oil is sometimes added to the wool to condition it which accounts for the black and greasy state of these bobbins when found.

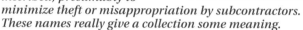

Some bobbins have the name of the manufacturer stamped on the flange or metal shield. The name of the textile mill that owned them was sometimes inscribed, presumably to minimize theft or misappropriation by subcontractors. These names really give a collection some meaning.

The name DIXONS can be found sometimes on bobbins originating from England. Dixons was one of the county's most prominent manufacturers, established in 1795 and in business up until 1983 in Steeton, Yorkshire, England. At its peak in 1926 it employed 425 people and during the life of the company made more than 3,000 different designs of bobbins.

Spinning bobbin from Saltaire Mill, England.
(see page 17)

FLYER SPINNING FRAME

Metal ends were fitted to bobbins to protect the wood and to protect the yarn from snagging. Some early metal shields in the damp atmosphere of the mills rusted and stained the yarn. From the middle of the 19th century, brass and copper were used. These bobbins are rare and very highly collectible. Later, steel was used because the copper and brass fittings were expensive to produce, but tinning or galvanizing helped to minimize rust.

Long Collar Tube

Ring Doubler

Some straight sided bobbins are off spinning frames.

Some of the larger bobbins have an unusual flared end below the flange, designed to reduce stress on the yarn as it is drawn off the bobbin in the drawing process. Some have only one flange and this also facilitates the flow of the yarn.

As a general principle, English twisting bobbins have a larger flange at the base and a narrow neck beneath the head.

Warping bobbins

BOBBINS USED IN THE WORSTED PROCESS

A great variety of bobbins are used in the spinning of worsted yarns. The draw-box being the largest, 14 and 16 inches in length and between 8 and 10 inches across the flange, followed by finisher or roving bobbins which measure 8 to 10 inches with 4 to 5 inch heads. The woolen yarn is more finely drawn onto small rover or reducing bobbins, 7 by 4 inches. The yarn is then further reduced onto a wooden single headed spool which is often capped with a metal protector. It is then wound onto a twisting bobbin.

The cap spinning method is used for spinning the longer woolen fibers used in the manufacture of worsted yarn. Cap spinning is an American invention which was copied the world over. It was invented by Danforth in 1830.

THE SIGNIFICANCE OF COLORED FLANGES

In past times, when workers were illiterate or immigrant workers had little communication, some mills color coded the machines and bobbins. Some of the large draw-box and roving/finishing bobbins have two colors, allowing a degree of flexibility.

In the last hundred years or so, color coding has generally implied different qualities of yarn in production at a mill, and not, as is often incorrectly assumed, different colors. This was most significant in the early blending process before spinning.

Cap Spinning Bobbin

Roving Bobbin

SCORING on bobbin barrels is caused by operatives removing unwanted yarn from them. To save time they often use knives, a practice generally forbidden in the mill, because sooner or later the body of the bobbin will become so rough as to be unusable.

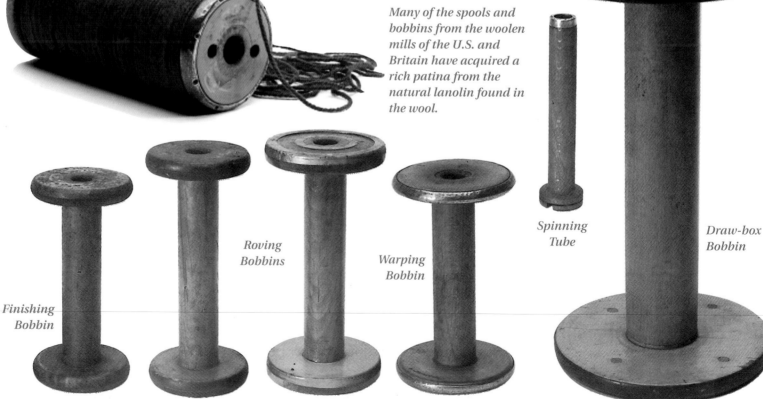

Many of the spools and bobbins from the woolen mills of the U.S. and Britain have acquired a rich patina from the natural lanolin found in the wool.

Finishing Bobbin

Roving Bobbins

Warping Bobbin

Spinning Tube

Draw-box Bobbin

General opinion is that bobbins with colored ends come mainly from the woolen industry. Mills color-coded their bobbins but with no attempt at standardization; each mill having its own system.

TWISTER BOBBINS

These add twist and strength to the yarn by combining two or more threads onto spools. Once again these come in a variety of sizes and vary according to the type of yarn being twisted.

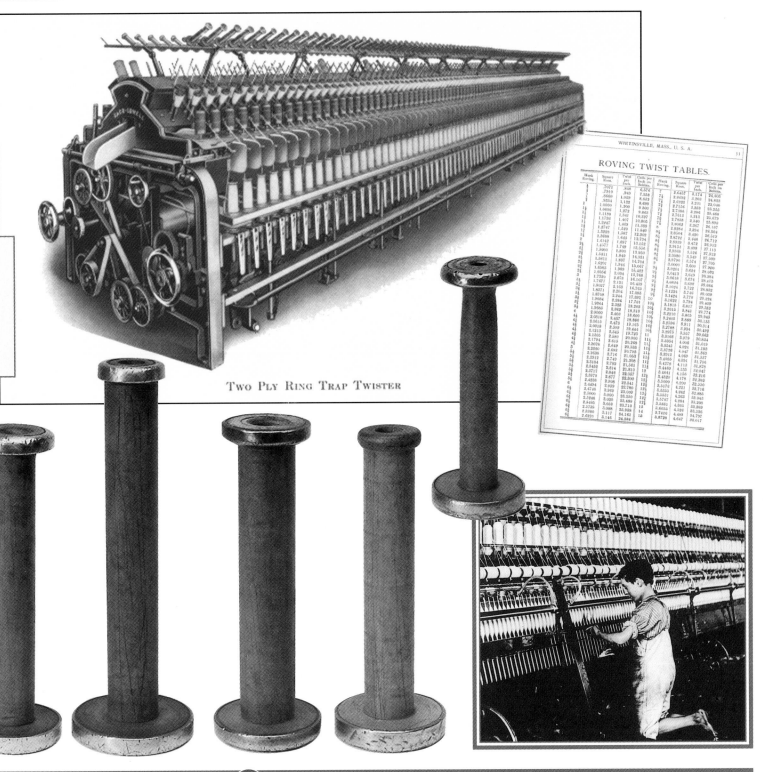

Two Ply Ring Trap Twister

FRAME BOBBINS

The typical frame bobbin measures 12 to 14 inches. The steps or ridges gave the yarn something to lock onto when a new run was started. These bobbins were used on creels on spinning frames. Their tops had to be smooth to prevent the yarn from snagging. They contained two brass ferrules; one at the base and one inside near the top. They took carded yarn from a jackspool, through the next spinning process onto the bobbin. Each bobbin was balanced and weighted if necessary. This variety of bobbin is found in a great many shapes and sizes, for different machines and different weights and thicknesses of fibers.

33

CONICAL RING DOUBLER BOBBINS.
Varnished all over only.

Standard Length of spindle	1¼" dia. and under	1⅜" dia.	1½" dia.	1⅝" dia.	1¾" dia.	1⅞" dia.	2" dia.	2¼" dia.	2½" dia.
6¼"	33/–	41/–	46/–	50/–	53/–	59/–	65/–	71/–	83/–	91/–
6½"	34/–	43/–	48/–	52/–	55/–	61/–	67/–	73/–	85/–	93/–
7"	35/–	45/–	50/–	54/–	57/–	63/–	69/–	75/–	87/–	95/–
7½"	36/–	47/–	52/–	56/–	59/–	65/–	71/–	77/–	89/–	97/–
7½"	37/–	49/–	53/–	57/–	61/–	67/–	73/–	79/–		
7¾"	39/–	51/–	55/–	59/–	63/–	69/–	75/–	81/–	91/–	99/–
8"	41/–	53/–	57/–	61/–	65/–	71/–	77/–	83/–	93/–	101/–
8¼"	43/–	55/–	59/–	62/–	67/–	73/–	79/–	85/–	95/–	103/–
8¼"	45/–	57/–	61/–	64/–	69/–	75/–	81/–	87/–	97/–	105/–
8½"	47/–	59/–	63/–	66/–	71/–	77/–	83/–	89/–		
9"	49/–	60/–	65/–	68/–	73/–	79/–	85/–			

Enamelled Black all over.

6¼"	50/–	58/–	64/–	68/–	72/–	79/–	87/–	93/–	107/–	119/–
6½"	51/–	60/–	66/–	70/–	75/–	81/–	89/–	95/–	109/–	119/–
7"	52/–	62/–	68/–	72/–	77/–	83/–	91/–	97/–	111/–	121/–
7½"	53/–	64/–	70/–	74/–	79/–	85/–	93/–	99/–	113/–	121/–
7½"	55/–	67/–	72/–	76/–	82/–	88/–	96/–	102/–	116/–	126/–
7¾"	57/–	69/–	74/–	78/–	84/–	90/–	98/–	104/–	118/–	128/–
8"	59/–	71/–	76/–	80/–	86/–	92/–	101/–	107/–	120/–	131/–
8¼"	61/–	73/–	78/–	81/–	88/–	94/–	103/–	109/–	121/–	131/–
8¼"	64/–	76/–		84/–	91/–	97/–				
8½"				86/–	93/–	99/–				
9"				88/–	95/–	101/–				

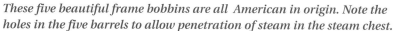
These five beautiful frame bobbins are all American in origin. Note the holes in the five barrels to allow penetration of steam in the steam chest.

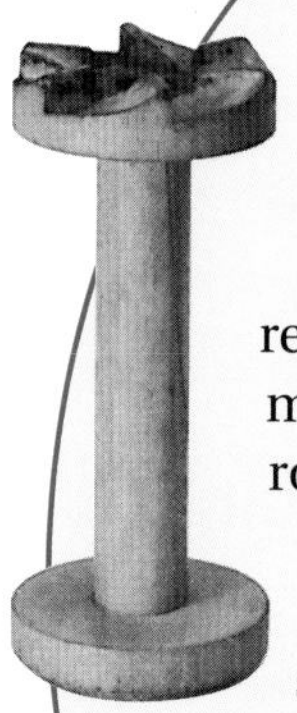

BRAIDER BOBBINS

The braider is a pretty bobbin, the base of which is notched or 'geared'. It is designed to fit onto a braiding machine, which in its action is reminiscent of the dancing patterns of maypole dancers who plaited ribbons round a central pole; once a common sight on village greens in England. These machines are used to make such items as shoelaces, decorative cord, washlines and certain ropes. Recently rugs and mats made of continuously spiralled braid have become popular in various shapes. Braider bobbins vary in size from 5 inches to 12 inches tall, depending on the weight and thickness of braid being produced.

Ring twisting machine with bobbins in position, two per spindle. Bobbins are ring spinners and have been transferred from the spinning machine for the twisting process.

SHUTTLE BOBBINS (QUILLS/PIRNS)

Shuttle bobbins, wound with yarn, are fixed into the shuttle, which then carries the weft thread back and forth across the loom. The designs are as many and varied as the shuttles. Those for the Northrop automatic loom are fitted with sleeves on the barrel. Earlier, they were aluminum and responded to an electrical mechanism when empty. Later, a reflective tape was introduced which triggered the mechanism optically. In this way the empty bobbin was replaced by a full one without the operator's intervention and without stopping the machine. The automatic bobbins have a three ringed gripper which is held in a calliper in the shuttle. Many quills are grooved along the barrel. These are designed to keep the yarn in place. Special bobbin-winding machines fill the shuttle bobbins at an amazing rate. Some machines are capable of winding up to 2,500 bobbins per hour.

CONES

These bobbins were used to store yarns for different operations. Cones with holes were used in the steaming operation to remove excess twist which made the yarn too lively to weave. This was especially important when dealing with certain springy man-made fibers.

STEAMER BOBBINS

It is still possible to find heavily lacquered bobbins which have holes running the length of the barrel. These were used when the yarn needed to be steamed to reduce excess twist. The lacquer kept the steam out of the wood which otherwise would have had a very short life. The holes allowed the steam to pass into the bulk of the wound yarn. Lively natural fibers sometimes need this to facilitate weaving. Perforated bobbins were also used in the dyeing process allowing the dye to be absorbed evenly throughout the yarn. Today metal perforated cylinders are used for this purpose. These are often referred to as 'dye tubes'

The Collector's View

For many of us it's enough that these items are beautiful to look at. But it doesn't end there. The vast collection of bobbins and spools created for 150 years throughout Europe and North America offers a wealth of history.

A collection consisting of all of the shapes representing spinning, for instance, makes a complete collection. Armed with this book, collecting from this angle is easy. Simply take a section and seek the range of styles. Now that bobbins and spools are distributed throughout the collector's market, they are available to the general public.

There is research information available in all major libraries about the textile industry. The various museums offer displays of equipment as well as history of the industry. Collecting bobbins and spools from the technical aspect can lead to exciting knowledge of our industrial past.

The woods used to make bobbins had to be hard, stable and extremely durable. The grains and colors of the woods are beautiful. The metals can be polished and buffed to their glistening brass, copper or steel finish. These elements are particularly eye-catching to both collectors and passing visitors.

The item is delightful and intriguing without changes, but simple embellishment with a touch of ribbon or sprig of flowers can add an artful look to a bobbin. For example, at Christmas time, red ribbons and berries trimming on the bobbins can add a festive look to a fireplace mantle. Moving the bobbins and decorating with summer flowers and a candle can give a new look for spring.

DISPLAYING A COLLECTION

All collectors want to share their passion by showing their display in an effective manner. Simply sort by style, color or wood, metal trim or any other way preferred. Depending on the size of the collection, bobbins can be grouped on shelves or mixed with other interesting collectibles.

Fireside hearth collection – shown on tile background. Bobbins fill a fireplace during the summer. Light the candles in the bobbins for a nice glow.

WHERE TO FIND BOBBINS...

They can be found in antique stores, collectible gift stores, flea markets, garage and yard sales, mail order catalogs specializing in antique items, and magazine ads.

You will probably want to display your bobbins and why not... they are so decorative; the different shapes, colors of woods, varied metals and so on. Bobbins are highly durable... great survivors! They had to be, so fragility is not something to worry about. They do hate damp though, and outdoors is not the place for them.

The 'technical' collector wants one of every style and shape for a period of time or for spinning or weaving, etc. The primary purpose is a complete collection of that specific group.

The 'decorator' collector appreciates the history of the items but enjoys primarily the ambiance created by a grouping of the spools, bobbins, and shuttles within a room setting.

A brick wall is a contrasting backdrop to bobbins collected on top of an antique butter churn for a county or primitive display.

Victorian table setting shows use of bobbins in elegant or dressy setting. Bobbins mix with all types of decor.

To group bobbins *technically*, simply line by style or size. To group *decoratively*, use the following guidelines:

a. *Groups of odd numbers work best in a circle arrangement for use on a wide shelf or on a table.*

b. *A range of sizes within the group is preferable.*

c. *A common element such as wood color, shape, or metal trim makes an attractive display.*

d. *These is no limit to location within the home or business for display of a group of bobbins. Use them anywhere.*

e. *Bobbins can be used to decorate with any style of decor from Contemporary to Classical.*

f. *Long shuttles or skinny bobbins can be placed on the surface horizontally in front of a standing grouping. The different angles add interest.*

g. *Slim or long bobbins can be stood vertically in a bucket, can, or wooden box, like a bouquet of flowers.*

Suggested Uses

The shape is reminiscent of candlesticks, so many people adapt the bobbins to hold a candle. This can be done by drilling a larger hole to match the candle size so it will hold it firmly. On bobbins with a flat end, it is easy to simply place a large candle or a candle cup with votive candle. If drilling is not preferred, simply reshape the candle.

A matched pair is a pleasing gift and can be the start of a collection for someone.

Bobbins can also be adapted to other useful, household items such as jump-rope handles, shelf brackets, and even bedposts! The wood turnings lend themselves to lots of imaginative uses.

Wrap thick, colorful yarn around the bobbin or spool. Wrap metallic yarns or fine copper wire for a glitsy look.

Place the bobbins in front of various textures such as a brick wall or a fireplace mantle, as illustrated on page 43, to highlight the texture and color of the woods.

Lay them in a basket with balls of yarn for color. Line the basket with a colorful cloth and cascade the bobbins over the side of the basket, standing a few alongside it.

A large bobbin serves as plant stand or pedestal for other items.

Bobbins are simply pleasant to own. The years they served the industry are now being rewarded with appreciation and a peaceful retirement. When something so utilitarian becomes respected for its age and its contribution to an industry, it is truly a collectible.

Pricing of bobbins is an inexact science. As with all collectibles, there is a gradual upward movement at work. There are several factors which are consistent in afffecting the value. Here are just a few . . .

Age – bobbins from primitive machinery, or with dates stamped prior to 1920. These can command high prices. Bobbins from the late 1800s will become very valuable

Metal trim – copper seems the rarest, followed by brass.

General condition – the smoothest with fewest cracks, scoring and dents seems to be more valuable.

Old patina – patina is the warmth, texture, and sometimes smell of an item. It is the "look" of an item that instantly invokes a response.

Paint – is often a misunderstood feature of a bobbin. Paint was used for identification in the mill – either for the type of yarn, type of machinery, or the batch of bobbins. The old oil paint applied to the ends becomes coated with lanolin and oil and it can also become worn away, further adding to the antique eye-appeal. This surface is impossible to duplicate. The old greens, blues and reds used at the time can be important decorating elements. All this said, there are many collectors who will pay more for bobbins which carry no color.

Fiber ends – were used from the 20s on. More bobbins of this period exist and were resistant to wear in the mills, so by the laws of supply and demand prices will be more modest. The colors used in the fibers; a deep red and a putty tan are perfect colors for antique decorating. Many have the same old patina as the all-wood bobbins. They can be a great buy.

LOOKING AFTER YOUR COLLECTION

Some of the bobbins will have already been carefully cleaned, oiled and polished before you find them, but even in shops they are sometimes offered for sale 'as found'. Just in case, here are a few tips.

1. Carefully remove excess oil and grime using a barely damp soft cloth, with a hint of liquid soap. As a much better alternative, denatured alcohol can be used as a cleaner and is widely available in hardware stores. Always observe the safety advice given on the container. Do not over-clean. It is the rich patina which gives the bobbin its character and antique quality.

2. Metal polish can be used on the shields, and buffed with a soft duster. If you are fortunate enough to find old tin shielded bobbins you may need to remove the rust with fine steel wool or a buffing machine.

3. The natural glow of the wood will be enhanced if the bobbin is coated with good quality oil. Lemon oil is recommended.

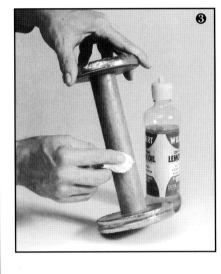

The Museum of American Textile History in N. Andover/Lowell, Massachusetts is a wonderful center for those in search of in-depth information.

A visit to the working museum at the Boott Mill in Lowell, Massachusetts provides a living mill experience for those wishing to sample the atmosphere of the past.

A bobbin lathe, among other working pieces of machinery, can be seen at the Slater Mill in Pawtucket, Rhode Island.

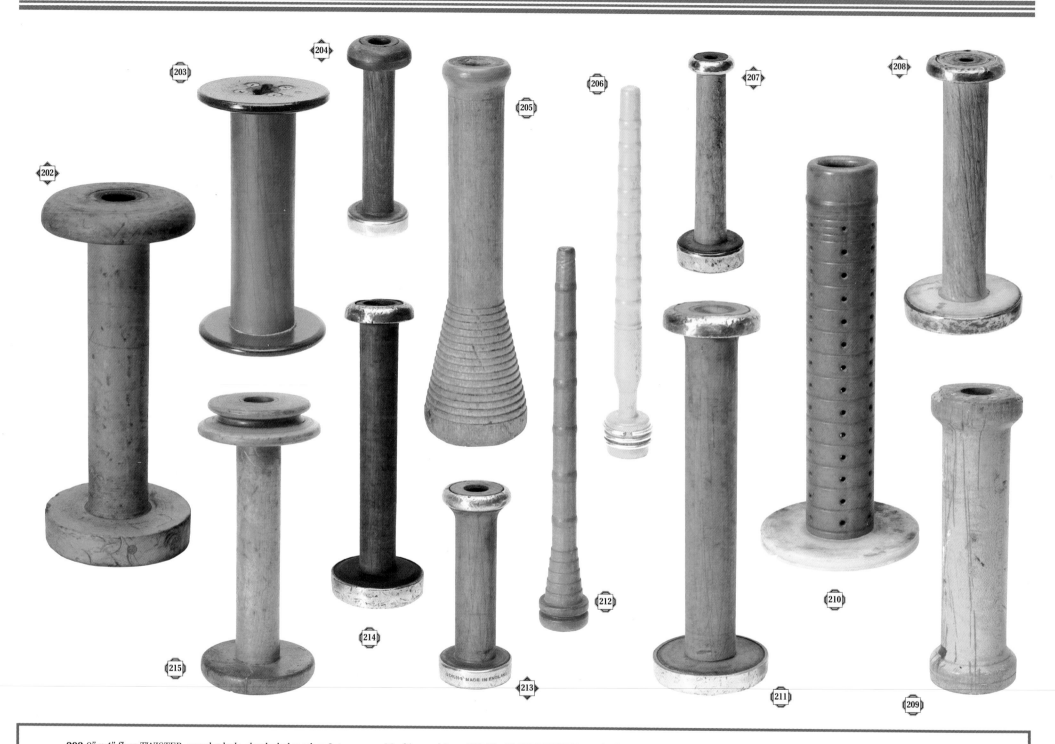

202 9" x 4" flyer TWISTER, speeder hole, dog holed washer. Jute or rope, Mackie machine. **203** 6" x 3" 10B TWISTER spool. Phenolic ends. **204** 5" CAP SPINNER ◇. **205** 10" FRAME bobbin for woolen yarns. **206** 8½" QUILL for heavy yarn. **207** 5" CAP TWISTER, c. 1875 brass top ◇. **208** 7" x 3½" TWISTER. **209** Yarn carrier for a doubler, 7" x 2", used to ply two yarns. **210** 10½" x 4" x 1½" paper tube, down TWISTER. **211** 10" x 3" x 2½" TWISTER, woolen yarn, brass. **212** 9" mule SPINNING bobbin. Ridged for wool. **213** 5" CAP SPINNER, brass, ◇ by Dixons. **214** 8" x 2½" novelty yarn TWISTER, brass. **215** 6½" x 2½" belt driven bobbin.

216 *12" x 6" x 5" TWISTER bobbin for wool or man-made fiber, with speeder hole and slotted washer.*   **217** *12" x 3¹/2" TWISTER ◯ worsted.*   **218** *7" silk QUILL.*   **219** *7" ring SPINNING bobbin.*
220 *5" CAP TWISTER, ◯ worsted.*   **221** *Barbara Coleman winder DYE TUBE 3¹/2" x 2¹/2".*   **222** *5¹/2" Abbott universal winder CONE.*   **223** *12" x 4" x 2" large package TWISTER spool. Brass ends.*
224 *9" x 4" ROVER/reducer/finisher bobbin, wool.*   **225** *7¹/2" x 3" TWISTER spool.*   **226** *8¹/2" x 3" x 2" copper ended novelty yarn TWISTER, heavy laquered.*   **227** *7" x 4" FINISHING bobbin.*

Raw Material to the Finished Product

Whether the raw material is plant or animal, the stages of production are very similar to achieve the transformation from many disorganized fibers to one single refined thread. The preparation prior to spinning may be different … wool needs scouring, flax needs retting, cotton needs scutching and so forth, but the next stages are so similar that machines and bobbins used in, for example, wool and cotton production can sometimes be difficult to tell apart.

WOOL

SHEARING of the sheep.

SORTING and SCOURING of the raw wool to clean and remove grease and other impurities. The wool passes through a series of washes.

BLENDING is an important stage in which wools of different qualities and natural colors are mixed together.

WOOL SORTS

"SHOULDER" wool is usually the best wool in the fleece. Next comes side, neck and back wool. The numbers show the order of preference.

Woolen Process
For wool in a wide variety of applications.

- SORTING
- SCOURING
- BLENDING — OTHER FIBRES
- DYEING
- PICKING
- CARDING
- SPINNING
- TWISTING
- (WARP) (WEFT)
- SPOOLING
- WARPING
- DRAWING IN — WINDING
- WEAVING
- BURLING & MENDING
- WET FINISHING (FULLING, DYEING)
- DRY FINISHING (NAPPING, SHEARING, PRESSING)

Worsted Process
For the specialized manufacture of worsted cloth – see weaving.

- SORTING
- SCOURING
- CARDING
- TOP DYEING — COMBING
- RECOMBING — DRAWING
- SPINNING
- TWISTING
- (WARP) (WEFT)
- SPOOLING
- WARPING
- DRAWING IN — WINDING
- WEAVING
- BURLING & MENDING
- WET FINISHING (FULLING, DYEING)
- DRY FINISHING (SHEARING, PRESSING)

A Scouring-Tank
Hot water and the action of the machine cleanse the raw wool to the accompaniment of a very pungent smell.

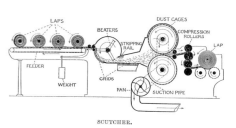

Even after the invention of Eli Whitney's cotton gin, the forerunner of the saw gin, the final cleaning of the cotton had to be done by hand. It was not until Neil Snodgrass of Glasgow invented the 'scutcher' in 1797 that this hand process became mechanized.

COTTON GIN FROM THE WAREHOUSE OF C. V. MAPES.

COTTON

The seed box of the cotton plant is harvested from the fields, packed into bales and delivered to the mill.

The weight of cotton picked in a day by each worker varies according to the skill and industry of the picker. It may be one hundred to three hundred pounds or more, but this is seed cotton; two thirds of the weight is seeds which come away from the plant with the fibers. These will be removed at the ginning stage.

Cotton Process

BLENDING & MIXING

OPENING & CLEANING

PICKING

CARDING

COMBING – – – DRAWING

DRAWING – – – ROVING

SPINNING

(WARP)   (WEFT)

SPOOLING

WARPING

SIZING – DRAWING IN

WEAVING

WET FINISHING
(DYEING, BLEACHING, MERCERIZING)

DRY FINISHING
(PRINTING, NAPPING, SHEARING, PRESSING)

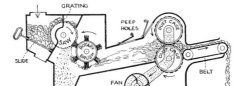

SECTION OF SAW-GIN

Early 1900s Breaking and scutching

SCUTCHER.

Blending – to achieve the uniform quality required.

Opening of the bales.

Picking or Scutching – the removal of seeds and dirt from the raw cotton.

Spreading – the formation of the cotton fibers into a flat sheet or lap.

228 15" x 2½" woolen, paper tube FRAME bobbin.   **229** 5" all wood CAP-SPINNER.   **230** Abbott universal 7" winder CONE.   **231** 4½" x 3½" warping or creel bobbin. Copper shields.   **232** 4½" BRAIDER bobbin.
233 4" silk creel bobbin. Mottershead and Co. Macclesfield.   **234** 4½" unidentified. Brass shields.   **235** 5" CAP-TWISTER.   **236** 11" x 8" Haskel Dawes ropemakers spool.   **237** 5½" CAP-SPINNER, brass shields.
238 10" TWISTER bobbin.   **239** 11" CONE: in-house yarn carrier.   **240** 7½" silk QUILL.   **241** 8½" x 3½" TWISTER ◇ worsted.   **242** 12" x 4" x 2" large package TWISTER spool.

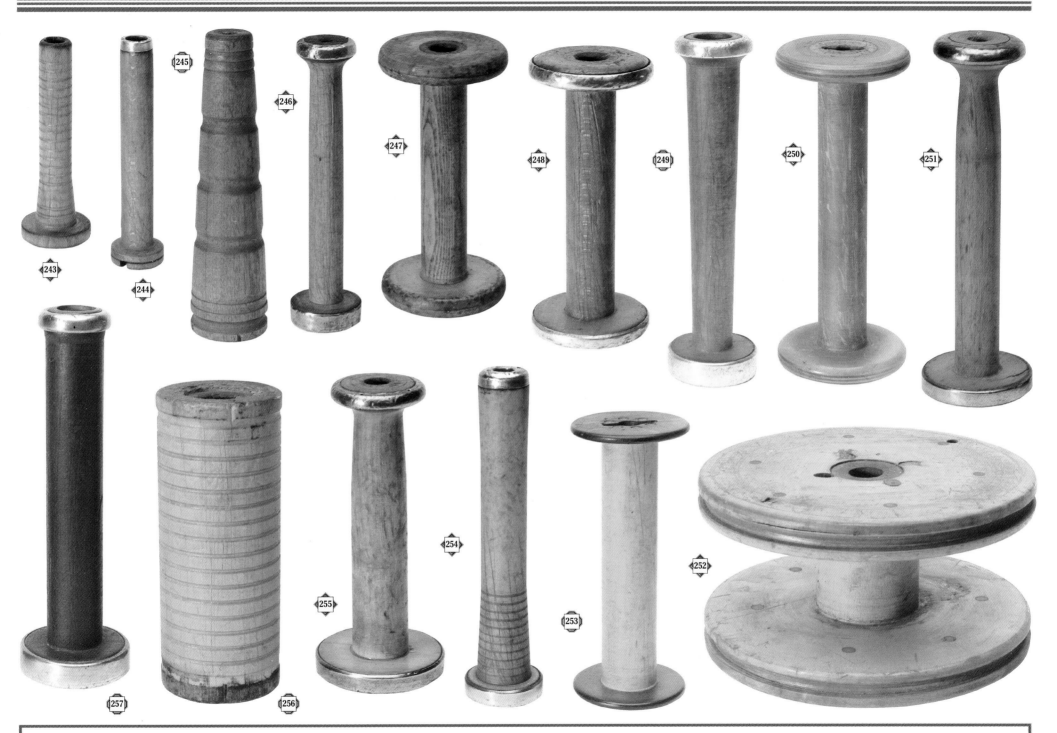

243 *5" sally TWISTING bobbin, ◇ with single flange.* **244** *5¹/2" SPINNING tube.* **245** *7" Abbott winder CONE.* **246** *8" x 2" TWISTER, copper top shield.* **247** *7" x 3¹/2" ROVING/reducing/finishing bobbin.*
248 *7" x 3" ROVING bobbin.* **249** *8" novelty yarn TWISTER spool.* **250** *9" x 4" ROVING bobbin.* **251** *10" x 3" x 2" TWISTER for mixed fibers, from France: mohair spinning.*
252 *4¹/2" x 8" selvedge bobbin, belt driven on the loom.* **253** *6" x 2¹/2" rayon TWISTER spool.* **254** *Cotton TWISTING bobbin. Arundel or Platts machines.* **255** *8" x 3¹/2" x 2¹/2" TWISTER.*
256 *7" x 2¹/2" heavy yarn CHEESE core: storage or carrier.* **257** *8¹/2" x 2¹/2" x 1¹/2" novelty yarn TWISTER spool.*

CARDING

Formerly a lengthy procedure done by hand but now carried out on a carding machine. This is the largest machine used in the industry. It consists of a series of large and small cylinders covered with tightly set wire teeth. The revolving cylinder teases out the fibers into a fine web of parallel strands. When the carding process is finished the fibers are scraped off the cylinder, emerging as something like an unwoven blanket. This is then condensed through a funnel into a soft rope, or SLIVER, which is allowed to coil downwards into a tall cylindrical container called a SLIVER CAN.

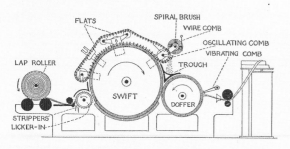

SECTION OF CARDING-ENGINE.

The carding cylinder was invented in 1748 by Lewes Paul. Its principle was developed with great success by Richard Arkwright, who patented a number of machines in 1775, for carding, drawing and roving.

Hand Carding Tools

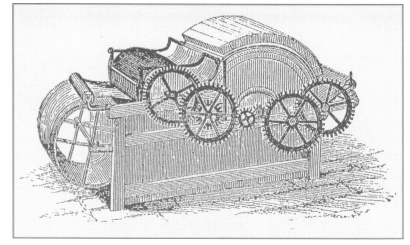

Carding Engine

The Reverend Edmund Cartwright, inventor of the power loom, patented the first combing machine in 1790.
Combing is a further refinement of the carded wool. Removing short fibers to achieve a high quality yarn.

IMPROVED LICKER-IN CARD.

This large carding machine, circa 1940, has rollers of various sizes running at different speeds and rotating in opposite directions so that the fibers are transferred from one to another.

Drawing- several slivers are gathered together from different cans and run through a set of rollers, typically arranged in four pairs. Passing through these, the fibers are drawn out into a new single sliver which paid into a can again. The drawing action is achieved by virtue of the fact that the pairs of rollers are revolving at different speeds. The second pair is revolving faster than the first, and the third faster than the second and so on, so the sliver is drawn out, and each time this happens the fibers are being further straightened.

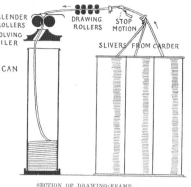

This process may be repeated several times, after which the sliver may be taken through a flyer or slubbing frame which both draws and twists, thereby adding strength and the resulting coiled rope of fibers is called a ROVING.

PREPARATION OF WORSTED YARN.

After being straightened, washed and dried, the short fibers are lost and the long ones are passed through a combing machine. The combed sliver is wound into a ball, called a top, ready for drawing and spinning. In recent years worsted-type yarns have been produced by the so-called semi-worsted system, which uses carding, gilling and spinning, but no combing. (Gilling is a process for drafting fibers and arranging them in parallel order, extensively used in the worsted system. Gilling is resorted to at various stages; after back washing, before and after combing, as a part of the drawing process.)

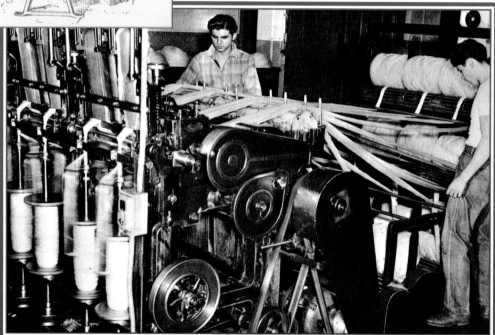

Scoured wool being fed into a carding machine

Slubbing frame

Slivers from several balls of top are being drawn and combined into one sliver and wound on spools.

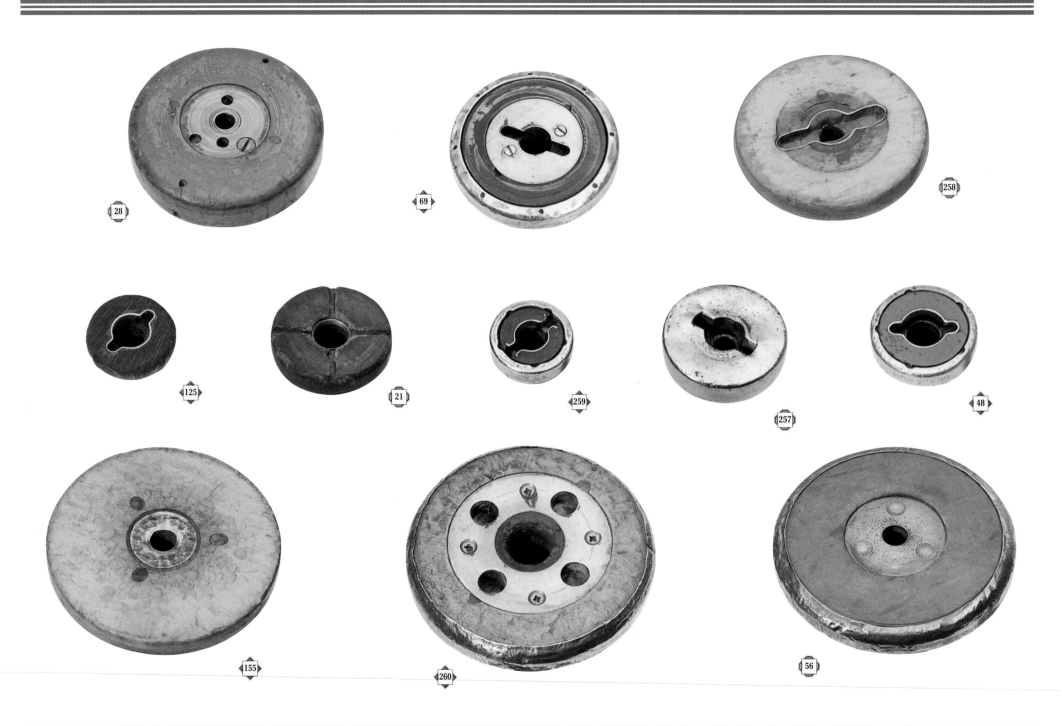

21 *Spinning FRAME bobbin; wool 12" x 2½" x 2".* **28** *6" x 4" rope-making spool.* **48** *CAP TWISTER 5½" with blue protective coating, brass core, copper shields.*
56 *11" x 6" shield cord TWISTER for Whitin twisting frame, wired for extra strength.* **69** *8" x 3½" x 2" perforated steamer/TWISTER ◯ copper and brass.* **125** *5" CAP-TWISTER copper top.* **155** *9" x 4" unidentified.*
257 *8½" x 2½" x 1½" novelty yarn TWISTER spool.* **258** *9½" x 5" x 3½" TWISTER, probably manufactured in England. Unusual having no shields.* **259** *5½" CAP TWISTER ◯ metal shields.*
260 *10 x 5" metal shields, for heavy yarn or articial fibers.*

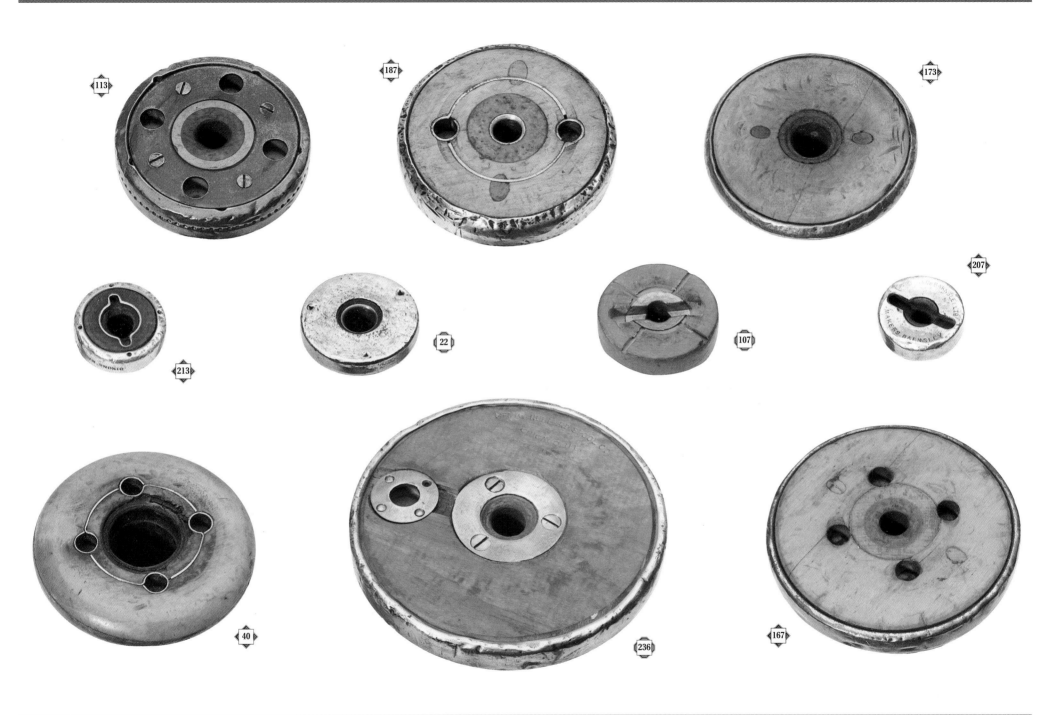

22 *Spinning FRAME bobbin, wool 12" x 2½" x 1½".* **40** *9" x 4" CONE ROVER with unusual drive fitting.* **107** *Cotton TWISTER, 9" x 3" Arundel or Platts machine.*
113 *9" x 3" cotton TWISTING. Arundel or Platts machine, bobbin by Wilsons.* **167** *9" x 5" ROVING bobbin by Dixons.* **173** *7" x 4" REDUCER or finisher bobbin.*
187 *9" x 4" brass ended, TWISTING, cotton or man-made fibers. Bobbin from Cromers Mill.* **207** *5" CAP TWISTER, c. 1875 brass top* ◇*.* **213** *5" CAP SPINNER, brass,* ◇ *by Dixons.*
236 *11" x 8" Haskel Dawes ropemakers spool.*

SPINNING

To make weaving possible, it is vital that the yarn has tensile strength. This is achieved by a process of twisting and drawing, known as spinning.

There are four types of spinning; Cap, Ring, Flyer and Mule. The mule system is used widely in French mills. The other three are used in English and American mills and are known as the Bradford System. America favored the cap system.

The degree of twist varies for yarns of different purpose; worsted yarn will have a 'hard' or tight twist, whereas softer twists will be worked into knitting wools

The spinning wheel appeared some time in the 1300s and was a great advance on what had been available before; a simple distaff and spindle. By todays standards, the production of yarn on a spinning wheel is lamentable, but this was nevertheless the only means available until 1765.

Spinning – when spun by machine, the same three sequences are necessary as in the old days of hand spinning.

Drawing – the stretching out of the fibers.

Importing a twist – the twisting of the fibers to ensure that they lock against each other.

Winding – the fibers are wound onto a bobbin so that they can be unwound for use in weaving.

PROGRESS IN SPINNING

The shortage of yarn brought about by the invention of the flying shuttle led inventors to search for something more productive than the hand-and-foot operated spinning wheel. In 1765 James Hargraves of Blackburn in Lancashire, England, invented the first practical spinning machine. The machine was named after his wife Jenny, who spun cotton thread in their cottage home. The original 'spinning jenny', can be seen in the Kensington Science

Museum in London, England. The big wheel was hand turned by the spinner., causing the spindles to rotate. The other hand pulled the bar at the front of the machine backwards and forwards. The resulting thread was wound around BOBBINS.

This new spinning machine was very popular and many were produced and used within the industry. Mill owners made fortunes by using it to spin cotton, but unfortunately for Hargraves, as is so often the fate of inventors, he was not to become a weathy man in consequence. Nor popular either, since his machine's productivity would inevitably threaten the lifestyle of the home-based spinners.

Designers tried to overcome the limitations under which spinning processes had previously worked – the need to rotate the package of yarn to produce twist. Break, or open-end machines, introduce a gap in the flow of the fibers, this overcomes the drawback and enables large packages to be made in a form suitable for weaving.

Thomas Highs, a reedmaker from Leigh, invented a spinning machine, which is believed to have been the inspiration for Richard Arkwright's famous invention.

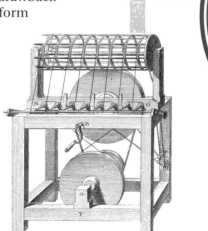

French spinning machine 1700.

Richard Arkwright, a one time barber turned wigmaker, was working on a different kind of spinning machine, which would spin four threads at once, drawing the threads with rollers and twisting them with flyers. Unlike the 'spinning jenny', Arkwright's frame had a continuous action which beckoned for the assistance of mechanical power beyond that of hand or foot. His first mill in Nottingham used horses, but a second built at Cromford in Derbyshire was driven by a waterwheel. From this prototype he developed what became widely known as the water-frame. This machine produced strong wiry yarn which spun excellent warp thread. The 'jenny' produced first class weft.

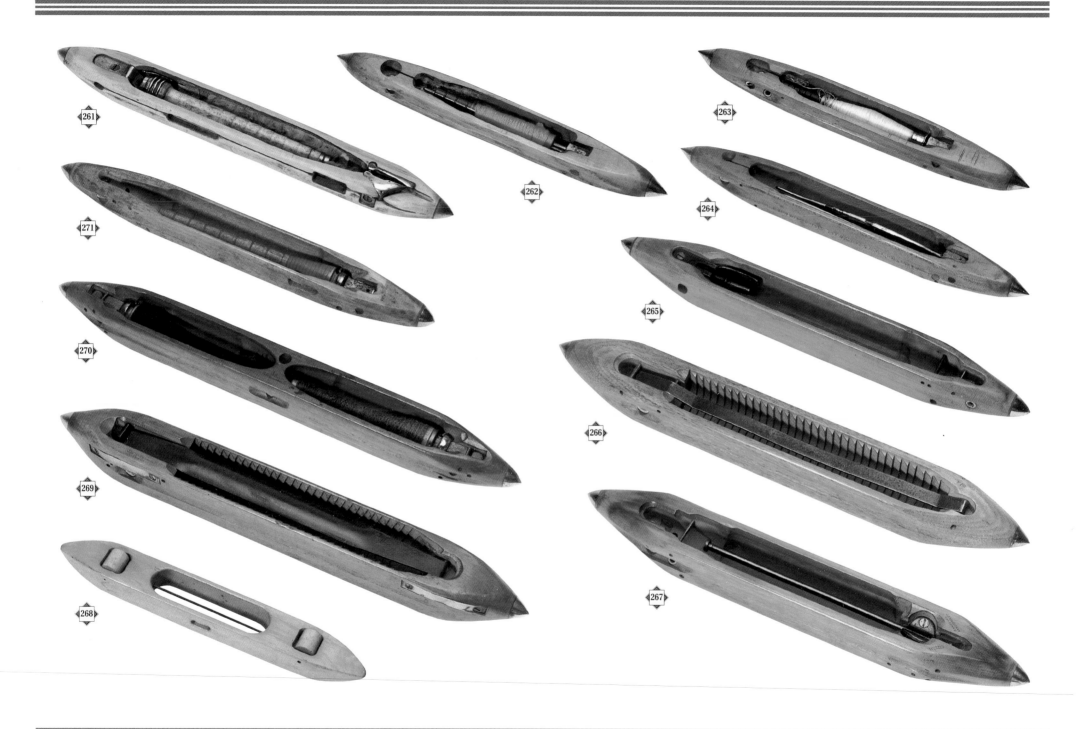

261 *Crompton and Knowles automatic silk shuttle.* **262** *Silk shuttle with "Courtaulds" type well.* **263** *Silk shuttle.* **264** *Manual-change cotton shuttle.*
265 *Woolen shuttle, persimmon wood, with jaw-cum-spindle for holding automatic quills.* **266** *Persimmon wood carpet quills.* **267** *A Hattersley loose spindle shuttle.* **268** *Handloom shuttle.*
269 *Persimmon wood carpet shuttle.* **270** *"Twin" handloom shuttle.* **271** *Manual-change cotton shuttle.*

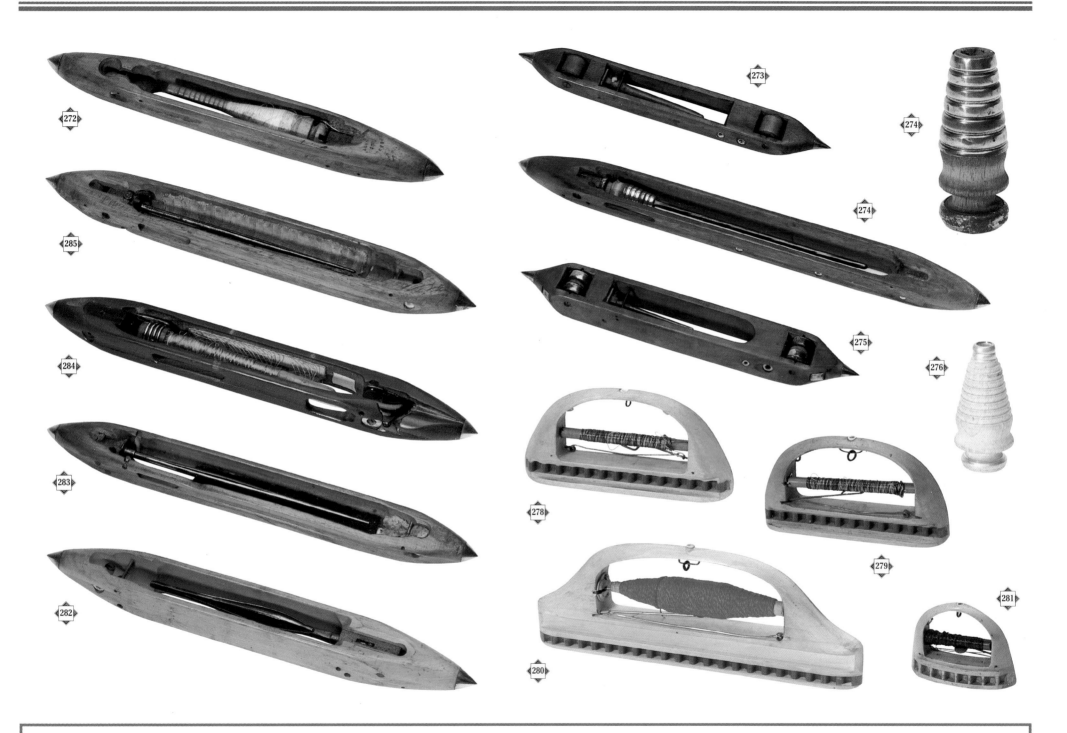

272 *Manual-change shuttle, cotton, with Universal pirn.* **273** *Handloom shuttle.* **274** *Velvet loom shuttle with supercop base.* **274a** *Supercop.* **275** *Handloom shuttle.* **276** *Supercop. (2½" long)* **278, 279, 280, 281** *Ribbon loom shuttles.* **282** *Manual change cotton shuttle.* **283** *Velvet loom shuttle.* **284** *Automatic silk shuttle (from underneath).* **285** *Manual change cotton shuttle.*

CROMPTON'S MULE

Inventors of the day were treated with suspicion at best and persecution at worst. For this reason Samuel Crompton, an inventor who lived near Bolton in Lancashire, was obliged to dismantle and temporarily hide a spinning machine he was developing.

Crompton was a specialist weaver of fustians (cloth with a linen warp and a cotton weft). The machine he had invented could produce very fine thread. He was so concerned about keeping his invention secret that he worked by night. Neighbors were curious and nervous about the strange noises which came from his home Hall i'the Wood. This gave rise to a rumor that it was haunted. Crompton's invention was called a MULE, because his machine was also a cross-breed, incorporating the characteristics of the spinning jenny and the water frame, and out-performing both. The mule was also known as the muslin wheel as it was capable of spinning very fine yarns. Crompton's mule was never patented so he received very little for releasing its secrets.

It was common for some mules to have up to 1,300 spindles in pairs. This mule was one of the last to be built in England by Platt Brothers in 1933.

MULE SPINNING C.1840

Thread from the bobbins at the top is passed through rollers and wound onto spindles at the front of the machine, in a measured length. Then the whole carriage (the part of the machine mounted on the wheels) moves towards the operator, while the threads of yarn are simultaneously twisted. This process is completed with the carriage at full stretch, and it then moves back while the twisted thread is reeled onto the lower spindles. Then the process is repeated with the next measured length. There is only just enough space for the millworker left to stand when the carriages of both machines are extended. An observer today, mindful of safety practices which we all take for granted, would find this a very alarming machine to see in action.

A MAJOR ADVANCE IN MACHINE SPINNING

1830 saw the introduction of an American invention of great significance. Ring spinning was introduced at the Merrimack Company, Lowell, Massachusetts. This machine, called a throstle, had sixty-four spindles. It derived its strange name from the noise it produced when it was operating. It supposedly resembled the song of the thrush.

The 'flyer' which had been used for three hundred years, was replaced by a metal ring around which a loop called a 'traveler' was drawn by a thread. This form of spinning quickly gained acceptance in the United States and was used for one hundred and fifty years but it was not until the 1950s that Britain adopted this much more efficient approach to spinning.

SECTION OF RING-SPINNING FRAME.

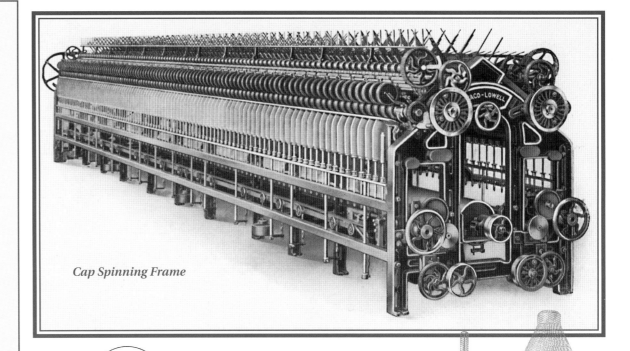

Cap Spinning Frame

RING SPINNING FRAME

Detail of Frame (Cap Method) Spinning. Roving (H) fed continuously from feed rollers (J) through spindles (L) which whip it around the cap (N), producing the required twist.
Caps (N) on innershafts (P), move up and down, control winding of yarn on bobbins (Q).

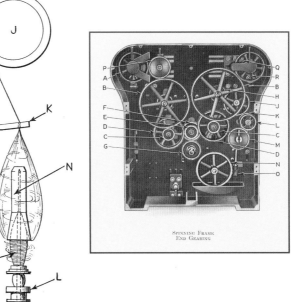

SPINNING FRAME END GEARING

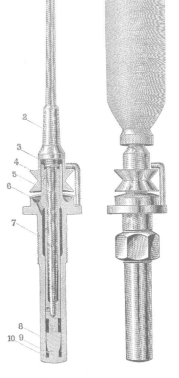

Gravity Spindle

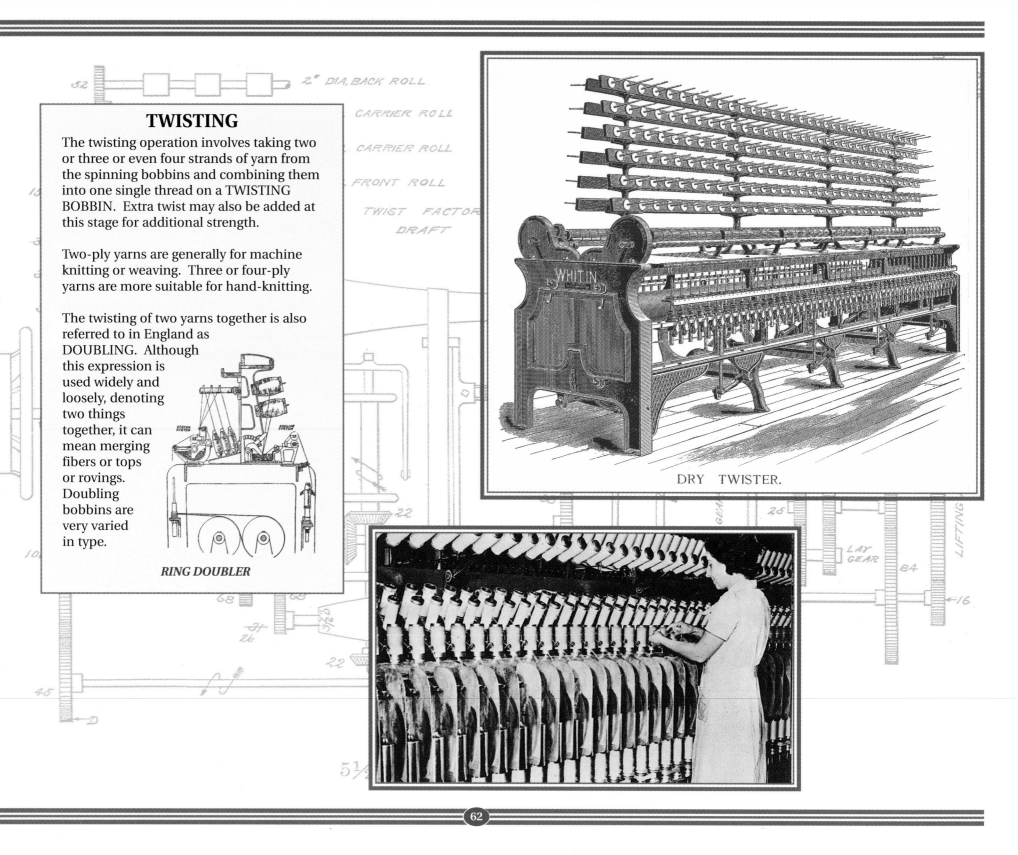

TWISTING

The twisting operation involves taking two or three or even four strands of yarn from the spinning bobbins and combining them into one single thread on a TWISTING BOBBIN. Extra twist may also be added at this stage for additional strength.

Two-ply yarns are generally for machine knitting or weaving. Three or four-ply yarns are more suitable for hand-knitting.

The twisting of two yarns together is also referred to in England as DOUBLING. Although this expression is used widely and loosely, denoting two things together, it can mean merging fibers or tops or rovings. Doubling bobbins are very varied in type.

RING DOUBLER

DRY TWISTER.

WHITIN

2" DIA, BACK ROLL

CARRIER ROLL

CARRIER ROLL

FRONT ROLL

TWIST FACTOR

DRAFT

WINDING or REWINDING

Rewinding has as its principal objective winding the yarn onto the bobbin necessary for the next operation. For examples:

If going to the dye house the yarn might be wound onto a stainless steel jackspool or dye tube.

Special bobbins for steaming the yarn were loaded for the steam chest. These might be heavily lacquered with thick heat-proof varnish, and would have non-ferrous metal shields, brass or copper, rather than anything which might rust. They would also have perforated barrels to assist the passage of steam through the body of tightly wound yarn.

If going to the weaving department, the yarn might be wound onto wooden cones. These would be mounted in big numbers on a creel from which they would be paid out onto a warp beam to build up warps for the looms. For the weft thread, pirns or quills are wound and fitted inside shuttles for the weaving process.

If used as out-of-house sale yarn, it might be wound onto inexpensive paper cones that would ultimately be thrown away after use.

The machine illustrated can wind 50 skeins at a time. Afterwards the skeins are removed and tied, either singly or as a double skein.

When the yarn leaves the twisting machines on a twister bobbin it goes to the REELING department. The bobbins are placed on a machine from which the knitting wool is unwound onto a SWIFT. This swift may be adjustable to produce a different size and length of SKEIN.

Light Running Reel

Saco Jack Spooler

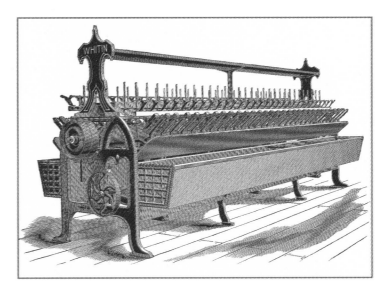

Whitin Spooler

PREPARATION FOR WEAVING

WINDING – The warp yarn (the thread that runs the length of the fabric) is wound onto bobbins that fit on a creel. This is a framework arranged to hold rovings of yarn so that the particular thread may be drawn off smoothly and evenly.

WARPING – From the creel, the warp yarns are wound onto a warp beam, each thread being coiled on top of itself so that when the whole beam is rotated the warp threads can be drawn out parallel to each other, through the loom.

DRAWING IN – Each warp thread is drawn through one or several heddles or healds. The heald will lift several threads at a time with the action of the loom. This will affect the pattern of the fabric. For every additional variation in the weave of the fabric, another heald will have to be employed. To fully appreciate the complexity and ingenuity of this process it is really necessary to watch a loom in action.

KNOTTING – The end of an expired warp thread is tied to another to save the exhaustive chore of re-threading through the healds once more.

By 1900 knotting machines speeded up this lengthy process. The Colman knotting machine is one example.

SIZING – A starchy substance is applied to the cotton warp giving strength and smoothness to the yarn.

To weave fabric, the warp and the weft were interwoven on vertical weighted looms.

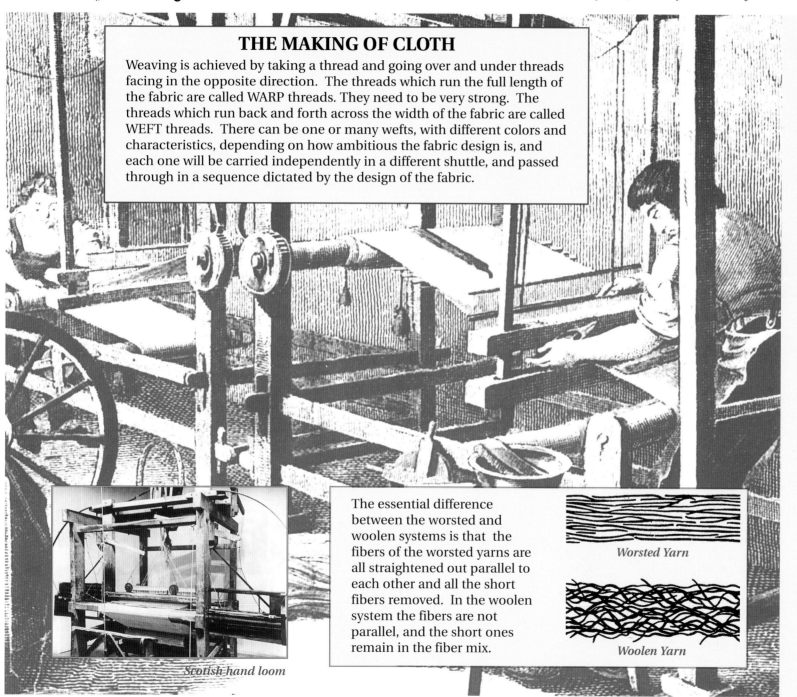

THE MAKING OF CLOTH

Weaving is achieved by taking a thread and going over and under threads facing in the opposite direction. The threads which run the full length of the fabric are called WARP threads. They need to be very strong. The threads which run back and forth across the width of the fabric are called WEFT threads. There can be one or many wefts, with different colors and characteristics, depending on how ambitious the fabric design is, and each one will be carried independently in a different shuttle, and passed through in a sequence dictated by the design of the fabric.

Scotish hand loom

The essential difference between the worsted and woolen systems is that the fibers of the worsted yarns are all straightened out parallel to each other and all the short fibers removed. In the woolen system the fibers are not parallel, and the short ones remain in the fiber mix.

Worsted Yarn

Woolen Yarn

The 1400s saw the appearance of horizontal looms. Immigrants from the Netherlands of Europe in the 1500s, favored the use of broadlooms in order to produce greater widths of fabric.

Inventions from the cotton industry were quickly adopted by the woolen manufacturers. By 1850, most worsted weaving was by power, but there were still handlooms at work in the woolen trade thirty years later. This was because woolen yarn, which has to be loosely spun, broke easily in the first rather clumsy generation of power looms. Later developments overcame these problems. Modern looms are now designed in which weft is speedily inserted by rapiers, grippers and air and water jets, making the old fashioned wooden shuttle redundant.

Narrow fabrics or tapes were produced on the Dutch ribbon loom.

THE DRAW LOOM

Until the 1500s Britain had produced largely plain woolen cloth, although some fancy weaving was carried out by specialist craftsmen in London and East Anglia. In the late 1500s Dutch and Walloon settlers greatly revitalized the textile industry in East Anglia, the first influx of Protestant refugees from Europe. The second wave was in the late 17th century when many thousands of French weavers from Lyon fled to England to avoid persecution. They settled in the Spitalfields area of London and brought new ideas and inspiration to fancy weaving. The draw loom which they used could produce beautiful cloth, highly colored and complex in design.

THE JACQUARD LOOM

The introduction of the Jacquard system was delayed in England because the ceilings of the weavers garrets were too low to accommodate them, but they could be introduced into the new mills. Now weavers were able to produce a greater variety of patterns, by the automated progress of the punched tape controlling the lifting of the warp threads in the correct sequence. Before this invention this task had been operated by hand by a child known in the trade as a 'drawboy'.

"Dobby" bar and chain when fed through a Dobby Loom in a continuous loop dictated the pattern of the cloth – a forerunner of the Jacquard system.

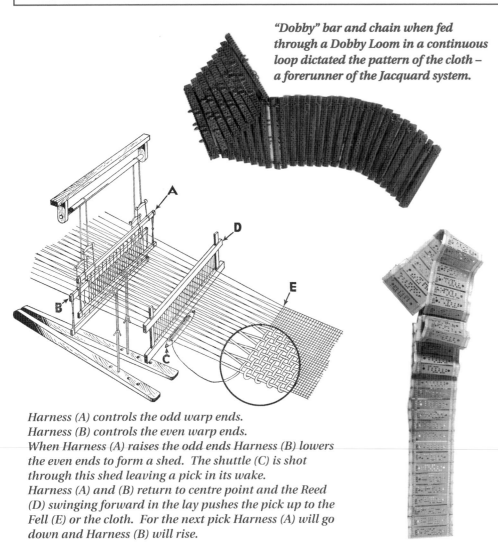

Harness (A) controls the odd warp ends.
Harness (B) controls the even warp ends.
When Harness (A) raises the odd ends Harness (B) lowers the even ends to form a shed. The shuttle (C) is shot through this shed leaving a pick in its wake.
Harness (A) and (B) return to centre point and the Reed (D) swinging forward in the lay pushes the pick up to the Fell (E) or the cloth. For the next pick Harness (A) will go down and Harness (B) will rise.

In 1725, a Frenchman by the name of Basile Bouchon, invented a selection device based on a roll of paper with punched holes.

It was Joseph Marie Jacquard who developed the idea, and incorporated a chain of pattern cards, an example of which is shown here (left).

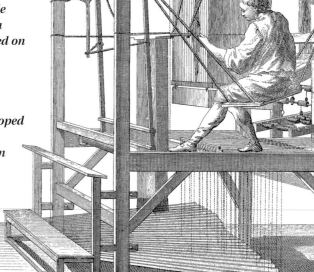

SIGNIFICANT STAGES IN THE MECHANIZATION OF WEAVING

In 1790 the first successful WEAVING MACHINE was made by a clergyman, Edmund Cartwright. Although his machine was completed in 1785, it was not until 1790 that he really made it work successfully. These early machines were very clumsy, and so even into the 1800s the handloom weavers still found plenty of employment.

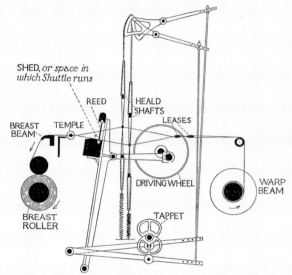

DIAGRAM OF THE ESSENTIAL PARTS OF A POWER LOOM

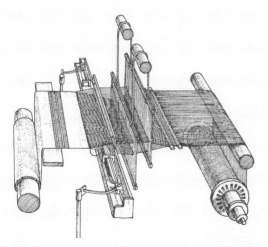

1733, John Kay invented the flying shuttle.

The Reverend Edmund Cartwright's Automatic Loom.

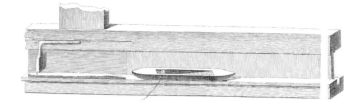

ILLUSTRATED CATALOGUE OF LOOMS.

MANUFACTURED AT THE

CROMPTON LOOM WORKS,
GEORGE CROMPTON, PROPRIETOR,
WORCESTER, MASS., U.S.A.
1876.

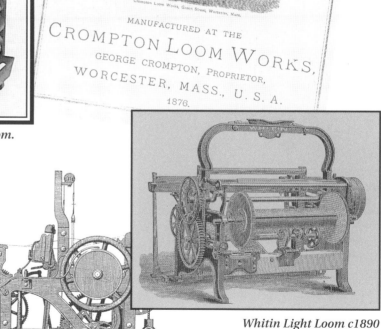

Whitin Light Loom c1890

Blackburn Loom c1830

DEVELOPMENT IN LOOMS

In 1840.Joseph Harrison, an ironmaster, produced a more refined and beautifully engineered loom. A leading authority on weaving said in 1978, "The early power looms were heavy and clumsy, but Messrs Harrison made such great improvements that the looms exhibited in the Great Exhibition of 1851(London, England) have perhaps never been surpassed."

In 1850, the Lancashire loom was perfected. It remained popular and reliable. Examples of this machine were still in use in the second half of this century.

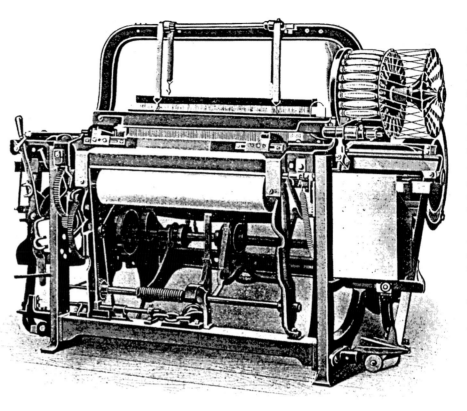

The widespread adoption of the Northrop Automatic Loom in America coincided with a shift of production from the northern states to the southern states cotton picking areas. By 1930, ninety percent of American looms were automatic compared with five percent in Britain. The southern states were the home of the raw material. There were numerous powerful rivers. Coal was mined in the Appalachian mountains, heating bills were lower, non-union cheap labor was available and there were tax advantages. It made good economic sense to move south.

THE AUTOMATIC LOOM

The first automatic loom was the 'Northrop' patented by the Draper Corporation of Hopedale, Massachusetts. Ira Draper, inventor of an improved fly shuttle hand loom in 1816, founded loom making in a cabin called 'The Little Red Shop', which still stands beside the firm's later foundry.

In 1894 James Northrop, an immigrant Yorkshireman, who had failed to interest the British in his ideas, went to work for the Draper Corporation. The principal innovation of his machine was the automatic transfer system which replaced the weft pirns in the shuttle without slowing or stopping the loom.

Miraculously, one weaver could now tend 16 looms. In time this would increase to 32. This remarkable loom quickly dominated the weaving industry, and was the first textile machine to be standardized. Any components which wore out could be replaced from stock. The Northrop loom was to become the Model T Ford of the textile industry.

In recent decades technology has dominated development. The shuttle is becoming obsolete; the weft now being inserted by rapiers, grippers and air and water jets.

Refinements to the Woven Fabric

Bleaching the woven fabric – Bleaching removes the natural creamy color of cotton making it white. It also cleans the cotton, removing any dirt and any oil picked up from the spinning and weaving process.

Burling – A finishing operation commonly used on woolens and worsteds, to improve the appearance of the fabric. It consists of removing objectionable knots, loose threads, etc., and is usually performed by hand.

Fulling (also known as felting or milling) – An important finishing process in the woolen industry. It depends upon the felting property of wool fibers and heat, moisture, friction and pressure are involved. These cause the material to shrink in length and width, lose its thready look and acquire a compact, substantial appearance and feel. Some fabrics are fulled so heavily that the weave and the yarns are entirely obscured and the material looks like felt. The fulling operation, which used to take days to complete, is now done by high-speed machinery. The old fulling stocks have been replaced by rotary milling.

Industrial Bleaching

Starching Machine

Bleaching

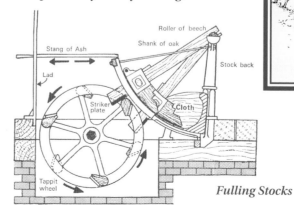

Roller of beech
Shank of oak
Stang of Ash
Stock back
Lad
Striker plate
Cloth
Tappit wheel

Fulling Stocks

Dyeing of wool – Wool may be dyed at various stages of production, but it is most commonly done as late as possible. When wool is dyed in its raw state after scouring it is said to be 'stock dyed'. The same process has given our daily language an expression implying something unchangeable … 'dyed in the wool'.

In a paddling mangle the cloth went through a trough of dye and then through a pair of rollers which squeezed out the excess dye.

It is common practice nowadays to dye quantities of YARN already wound onto metal bobbins, called dye tubes.

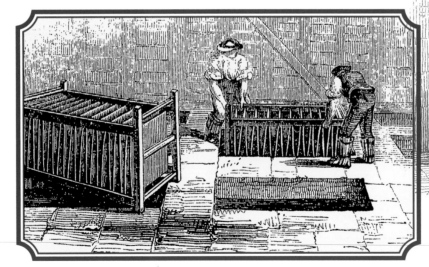

In the early 19th century cloth pieces were dyed with indigo by dipping them in and out of a dye vat. By the end of the century a rope of cloth was being drawn continuously through a series of dye troughs.

After dyeing, steam was used to fix the color on to the cloth in a steaming cottage. Later in the century continuous lengths of cloth were treated in steaming or ageing machines: steam from a boiler was directed over the cloth as it was drawn over heated rollers.

PRINTING THE WOVEN FABRIC

Hand blocking, or printing with the use of carved wood blocks, is still to be seen commonly in India, but the introduction of printing rollers in the late 1800s brought printing into line with the speed of mass production. Rollers, like the hand blocks which preceded them, were highly intricate in their manufacture and immensely expensive to make, often being inset with brass for the fine detail, and one roller being required for each color of the pattern.

Block Printing

CLOTH MADE AND PRINTED BY THE

MERRIMACK MANUFACTURING Co.

LOWELL, MASS.

W

INCORPORATED 18

Warranted Fast Colors.

Napping – A finishing process which raises a nap on the surface of the cloth. The cloth, in a tightly stretched condition, is passed over a rapidly revolving cylinder covered with prickly wire matting or set with TEASELS. The teeth of the wire or teasels prick the threads and raise the nap which is the fibrous surface of the cloth. A TEASEL is the dried seed box

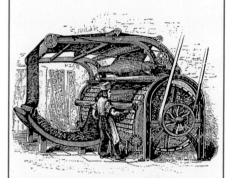

of a plant, Dipsacus fullonum, which is covered with stiff hooked prickles and used for raising the nap of the cloth. It is cultivated in Oregon, New York and Southern France for this purpose.

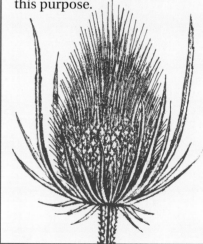

The Silk Industry

For over two thousand years, silk came only from China. The Chinese fiercely guarded the secrets of silk production from the Western world. This very desirable fabric was exported by the Chinese along the six thousand mile 'Silk Route' through Japan, Korea, India, the Middle East and finally to Europe.

In the eighth century, 'sericulture' (the art of breeding and raising the silk worm) was established in the warmer Mediterranean countries; Spain, Greece and Italy.

The British climate was far too cold for the breeding of silk worms. However, a small silk industry developed in England during the 1400s, with expertise brought by skilled immigrant workers from the Netherlands and France. In the early days of silk production in England, ready thrown silk had to be imported from Italy. (Throwing is the process by which raw silk is wound from the skein, twisted, doubled and twisted again.) Macclesfield in England evolved as the center of the British silk industry.

French silk ribbon making, c1700.

Silk bobbin from 20th century machine

Doubling 1830

John Ryle, 1817-1887, started his working life as a bobbin boy in Macclesfield, England. At the age of 22 he became his brother's agent in New York. He moved to Paterson, New Jersey and established a silk business. During this period the British silk industry was suffering a serious decline. Ryle campaigned for restrictions on imports to the U.S. of silk fabrics, and this helped to ensure the success of the Paterson plant. It was a challenging time for the English silk workers, with few alternative employment prospects. Whole families looked to the growing silk industry in the U.S., and it was America's turn to benefit from an influx of skilled immigrant labor. The coat of arms of Paterson N.J., shows a worker planting a mulberry tree, the leaves of which provide the staple diet of the silk worm.

Later, the American silk industry was to move from Patterson New Jersey to Pennsylvania for both tax purposes and to use farmers' wives for workers.

Belding Bros. & Co. Silk Mills, Rockville, Conn., c. 1876.

Silk weaving room – Famous Silk Mill, Paterson N.J.

Silk weavers' cottages, Macclesfield, England

Macclesfield in England and in the U.S., Paterson, New Jersey, were the chief centers for silk powerloom weaving in their respective countries, but the silk market today is dominated by goods produced in the Far East and the Pacific Rim.

THE PRODUCTION OF SILK FROM SILK WORM TO FABRIC

The silk thread is usually removed from the cocoon in the country of origin. The cocoons are placed in a bath of warm water which softens the gum, seracin, and the ends of the threads become detached. Two groups of threads are gathered together from several cocoons, and wound onto swifts, which are star-shaped skeleton reels constructed of lancewood. Then the skeins are removed from the reels. They are then color coded with temporary dyes and placed in groups of three forming a 'moss'. Twelve mosses form a book which weighs about 10 pounds.

The raw silk is now ready for throwing. This incorporates several processes – winding, cleaning, spinning and doubling as well as the throwing itself. Throwing is the process of doubling and twisting the silk thread into a yarn of the desired denier in preparation for weaving.

Throwing 1850

Silk, in its raw state, is the product of the silk moth during the caterpillar stage in its life cycle, when it is referred to as a silkworm.

There are many varieties of silk moths in the wild but the one most widely used for 'sericulture' (the manufacture of silk) is the **Bombyx mori**, a moth of $1^{1}/2$" wingspan, and relatively small compared to the Tussah silk moth of India which measures 6".

In the controlled conditions of sericulture, eggs are laid on trays which are set out on cards when they are ready to hatch. Mulberry leaves will be the food for the caterpillars which eat night and day for 3 to 4 weeks and achieve 3" in length, shedding their skin four times on the way. When they are ready to change into pupae loose twigs are laid over them onto which they will spin their cocoons.

The silk is formed in a pair of glands and flows out of openings on the worm's lower lip called 'spinnerets', hardening as soon as the air gets to it. The threads on the outside of the cocoon are twisted and rough but those on the inside are smooth.

When the worm has completed its cocoon, man takes over again. It is placed in dry heat to kill the pupae inside, and then into warm water to soften the gummy substance called 'seracin' which adheres the silk to itself. The rough outer silk is removed. (This will go to the silk waste spinning industry for processing, to produce spun silk fabric; a material of lesser cost and quality than 'raw' silk.) The stripped cocoons are then selected for unwinding onto reels. Two groups of thread are gathered together, each group containing from three to twenty cocoon threads and are wound onto square reels. This is usually performed in the country of origin and the resulting skeins of raw silk may then be exported to a silk throwing mill for further cleaning, spinning, doubling and throwing. The finished thread may then be used for sewing or weaving.

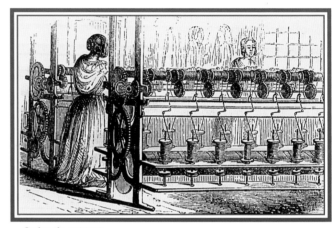

Spinning 1850

Winding silk

Silkworm eggs are bought and sold by weight. One ounce will contain around 35,000 eggs.

MACHINES IN THE SILK INDUSTRY

The first centers of silk weaving in Britain were Spitalfields, Canterbury, Coventry and Norwich. The earliest date back to the 1400s. The first silk looms in Britain produced narrow braids and single ribbons. In the early 1600s refugee weavers from Holland introduced a hand operated machine which could weave up to twelve pieces of ribbon simultaneously. Its twelve parallel shuttles moved by cogwheels. The first powerlooms in the silk industry produced ribbons. They were introduced in the early 1800s and called NARROW LOOMS.

In 1721, Thomas Lombe introduced the Piedmontese throwing machines into his new silk mill in Derby. These machines of Italian invention were circular and up to nineteen feet high with a diameter of 12 to 15 feet. They occupied two floors of the silk mill. An inner cage, activated by a central vertical shaft, caused the spindles on an outer cage to revolve. These amazing wooden machines were replaced in the early 1800s by smaller machines constructed of metal, with finely turned steel spindles instead of cast iron. They took up far less room and worked at higher speeds.

In 1771, Thomas Crawford invented the power-driven wooden doubling frame, later to be constructed of metal.

In 1851, Frost of Macclesfield produced a spinning/doubling machine which combined two processes, saving time and money.

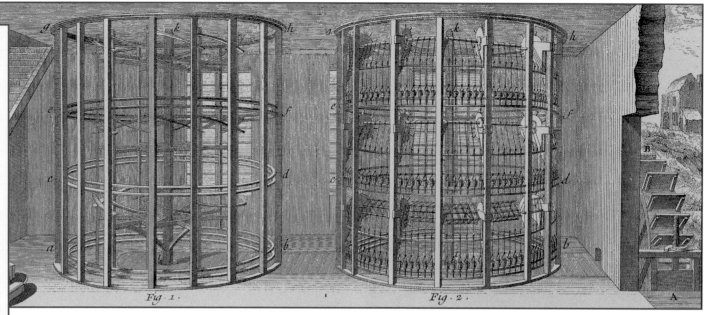

A Piedmont mill, mechanization of twisting and doubling. Silk Mill Italy, c1700.

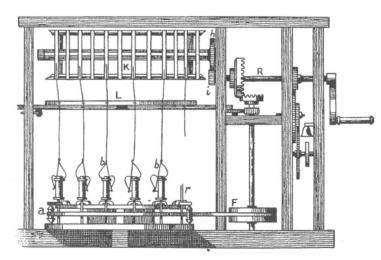

Small oval hand-operated throwing mill c.1800.

The drawloom was first introduced to Britain by immigrant refugees from the Low Countries in the 1500s. By 1820 the industry saw the first Jacquard selective looms adopted into use. A factor delaying earlier adoption in Britain was the fact that the weavers garrets were too low to house the new looms. The Jacquard required a clearance of eleven to twelve feet.

It was not until 1830 that power looms for broad silks were first used. They were introduced by Courtauld's in their factory in Essex.

In 1838 a patent was granted for a Jaquard machine attachment to the powerloom.

In 1878 the velvet loom invented by Reixach was patented by Samuel Lister of Manningham Mills, Bradford.

By the end of the Second World War, the rapier loom had been introduced. In this machine the shuttle was replaced by two hooks which met in the middle and passed the weft from one to another. For broadloom weaving the rapier is still the most popular loom used today.

SHUTTLES

The first major technical innovation in the 'modern' textile industry was the FLYING SHUTTLE. This was invented in 1733 by John Kay, a professional weaver. Before this, the shuttle had to be thrown across the loom by hand, so the width of the cloth depended upon the width of the weaver's arms. Now, instead of being thrown, the shuttle was driven along a wooden groove by small hammers. The hammers were operated by strings.

Ribbon Shuttle

Shuttles had to be very strong to withstand the battering as they were propelled with speed across the loom. They had to be made out of the finest tight-grained hard-woods, crafted and finished by hand to a very high standard in order to protect the fine yarns from snagging. The pirn wound with yarn is neatly situated in the center of the shuttle.

WILSONS OF ENGLAND

The early English shuttles had been made of alder, birch and hazlewood, but now harder woods were required. The textile manufacturers in England and America took out a franchise on areas of forest in South America. Persimmmon, boxwood, lignastone and cornel were harvested. Trees which grew high on the hillsides were superior, being slower growing and with finer grains and fewer knots because of shortage of water. It is these magnificent and practically indestructible shuttles which are the focus of the collector's attention today.

As sometimes happens with new inventions, Kay's machine was unpopular with the workers, who felt pressured by the greater output required of them, as well as the short supply of spun yarn, bringing fears of unemployment. John Kay was forced to leave Colchester where he lived and worked and move to Bury in Lancashire. In Bury he was to find no peace from the mob; his house was attacked by angry workers, his life was threatened and he fled to France.

BOBBIN, SHUTTLE, AND CHEMICAL WORKS
GARSTON, LIVERPOOL, ENGLAND

A shuttle carries the wound shuttle bobbin (pirn or quill) across the loom releasing yarn as it flies between the warp threads. Many are designed slightly off center to prevent them flying off the sley of the loom when operated at high speed.
The ends are tipped with strong protective metal cones, giving them a bullet like appearance. These tips become extremely hot in use.

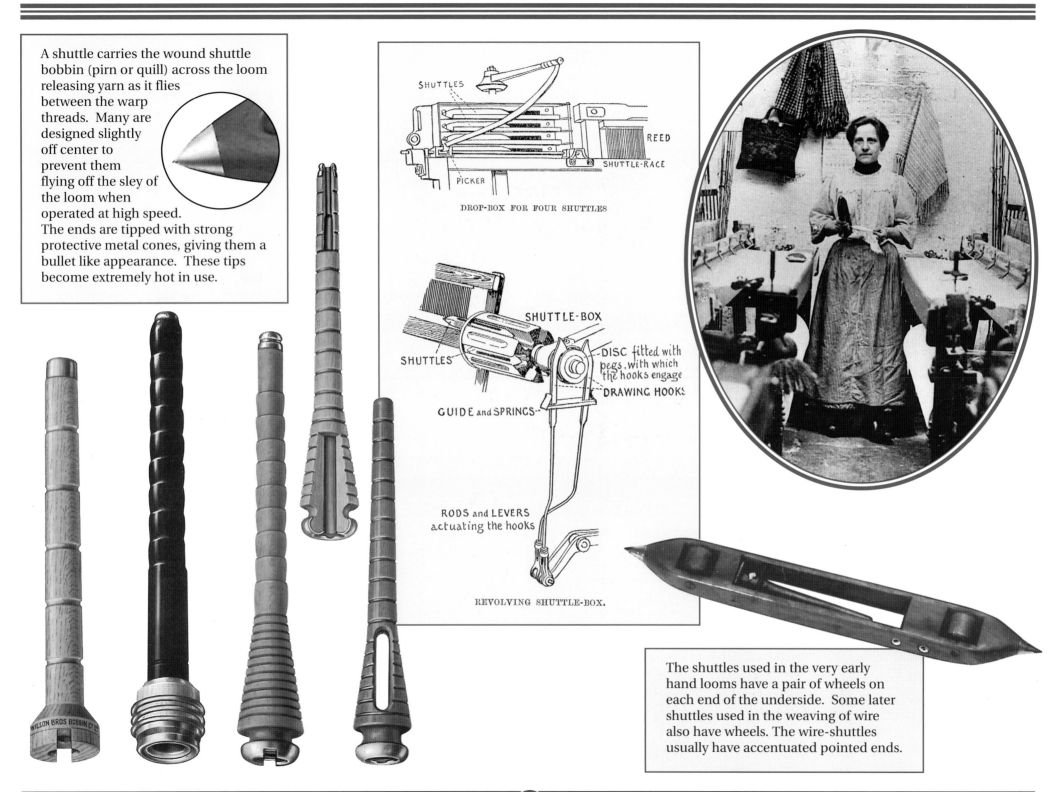

SHUTTLES

REED

PICKER

SHUTTLE-RACE

DROP-BOX FOR FOUR SHUTTLES

SHUTTLE-BOX

SHUTTLES

DISC fitted with pegs, with which the hooks engage

DRAWING HOOKS

GUIDE and SPRINGS

RODS and LEVERS actuating the hooks

REVOLVING SHUTTLE-BOX.

The shuttles used in the very early hand looms have a pair of wheels on each end of the underside. Some later shuttles used in the weaving of wire also have wheels. The wire-shuttles usually have accentuated pointed ends.

Shuttles carrying the automatic shuttle bobbins have open slots on the sides and an open base through which the empty pirn can be ejected.

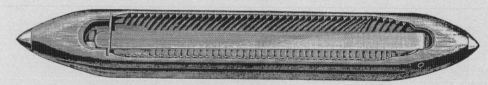

Early shuttles were fitted with a porcelain eye through which the thread had to be sucked by mouth. These became known as 'kissing' shuttles, because that is what the weaver appeared to be doing. This practice was discontinued when medical knowledge advanced and it became accepted that the inhalation of dust and residual oils from the fibers caused cancer of the mouth and lungs. The kissing shuttle was renamed with the grisly nickname of 'The Death Shuttle'. The use of these shuttles is long condemned in the Western world although some are still believed to be in use in Third World countries. Many shuttles could be, and were, more safely threaded using a small, metal shuttle threading hook.

In most shuttles the yarn is fed through an eye or series of eyes at one end of the shuttle. This controls the tension of the yarn.

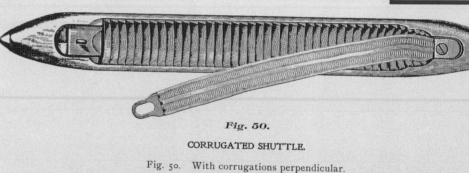

Fig. 50.

CORRUGATED SHUTTLE.

Fig. 50. With corrugations perpendicular.

Fig. 47.

CORRUGATED SHUTTLE.

No spindle. For cop-filling yarn (see Figs. 205 and 217).

The size of the shuttle is generally an indication of the thickness of the yarn being woven. The interior of shuttles for heavy carpet wools are ridged and the yarn is woven onto a small wooden 'cop' instead of a 'pirn' or 'quill'. Consequently the wound yarn has no solid support up the center, so the ridges carved in the body of the shuttle, together with a wide metal or canvas strap along its length, served to hold the yarn in place.

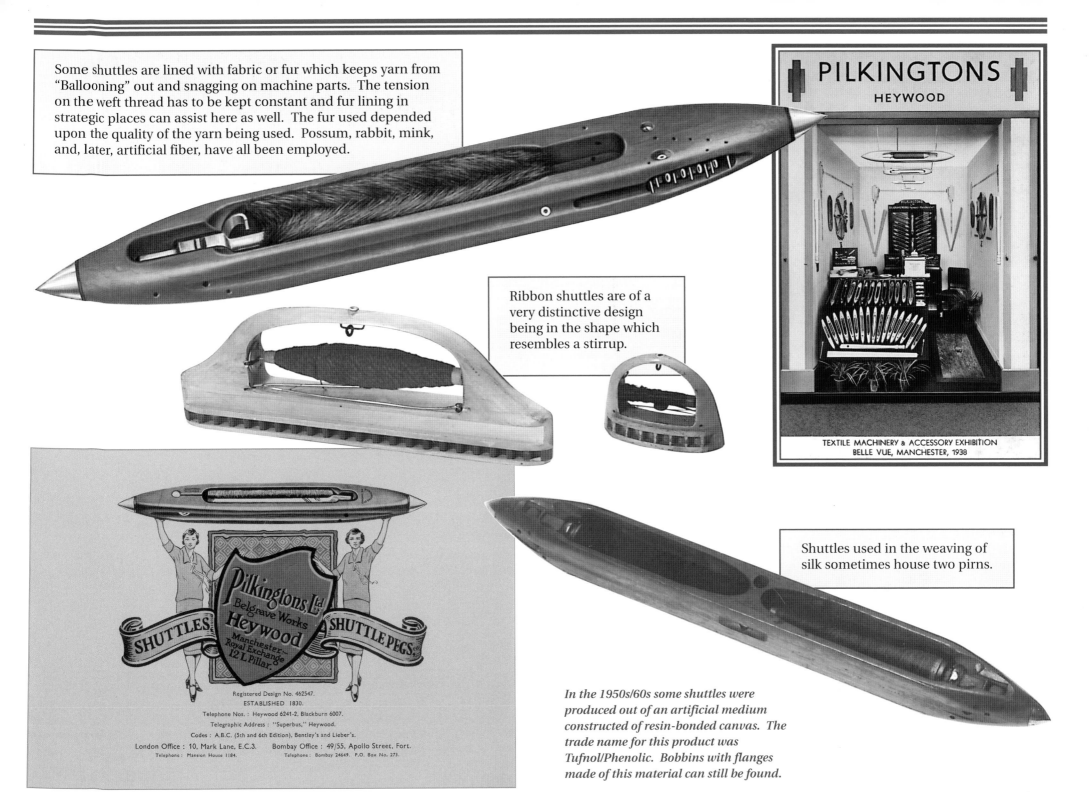

Some shuttles are lined with fabric or fur which keeps yarn from "Ballooning" out and snagging on machine parts. The tension on the weft thread has to be kept constant and fur lining in strategic places can assist here as well. The fur used depended upon the quality of the yarn being used. Possum, rabbit, mink, and, later, artificial fiber, have all been employed.

Ribbon shuttles are of a very distinctive design being in the shape which resembles a stirrup.

PILKINGTONS
HEYWOOD

TEXTILE MACHINERY & ACCESSORY EXHIBITION
BELLE VUE, MANCHESTER, 1938

Shuttles used in the weaving of silk sometimes house two pirns.

Pilkingtons, Ltd.
Belgrave Works
Heywood
Manchester—
Royal Exchange
12 L Pillar.
SHUTTLES   SHUTTLE PEGS

Registered Design No. 462547.
ESTABLISHED 1830.
Telephone Nos.: Heywood 6241-2, Blackburn 6007.
Telegraphic Address: "Superbus," Heywood.
Codes: A.B.C. (5th and 6th Edition), Bentley's and Lieber's.
London Office: 10, Mark Lane, E.C.3.   Bombay Office: 49/55, Apollo Street, Fort.
Telephone: Mansion House 1184.   Telephone: Bombay 24649. P.O. Box No. 273.

In the 1950s/60s some shuttles were produced out of an artificial medium constructed of resin-bonded canvas. The trade name for this product was Tufnol/Phenolic. Bobbins with flanges made of this material can still be found.

GLOSSARY

BAR AND CHAIN see Dobby.

CARDING disentangles and removes most of the impurities from the raw material fibers, presenting the maximum useful amount in a manageable and parellel form called a 'sliver'.

COMBING is a selective process where the fibers are literally combed in a machine, removing fibers below a desired length. This can be wasteful of raw material and so is generally employed in high grade work; fine or high quality yarns.

COP a cigar shaped package of yarn that rides inside a shuttle. Name also applied to a tiny spinning top-shaped bobbin on which the 'cop' is wound.

CREEL a frame holding a number of bobbins of yarn.

DOBBY this resembles a ladder-like construction of wood and metal which is attached to a loom enabling a progam to be selected. Also called bar and chain.

DRAFTING OR DRAWING OUT is the thinning and lengthening out of a rope of fibers.

DRAW BOX a machine on which the 'roving' is drawn out.

DRIVE PLATE this is a metal device on one end of a bobbin which drives the bobbin.

DUCK SHUTTLE a shuttle which is designed to carry medium and heavyweight yarn for the production of tough fabrics – those for example, which are used in the manufacture of army uniforms.

FEELER (OPTICAL) a device which senses an empty pirn and ensures its replacement in a Northrop automatic shuttle.

FIBER (when referring to bobbin construction) vulcanized or compressed paper or other patent material.

GINNING removing seeds from cotton fibers.

GRIPPERS are the rings on the head of a quill by which it is gripped within the shuttle.

JACQUARD a machine added to a loom which can be programmed to select and lift individual warp threads in order to produce patterned fabric. Forerunner of the computer.

LAP a single layer of cotton fibers wound in sheet form round a roller.

PACKAGE a cone, bobbin or 'cheese' of yarn or roving.

PHENOLIC a patented material, frequently buff colored, pinkish or green. Not unlike Bakelite, one of the forerunners of plastic and common on bobbin ends from the '40s onwards.

PICKER usually a tough buffalo hide block which hits and propels the shuttle across the loom.

PICKER STICK the stick which propels the shuttle.

PIRN (or quill) a tube on which weft thread is wound and which fits into a shuttle.

QUILL a light, slender tapered tube upon which filling yarn, is wound before weaving. Similar to pirn.

RAPIERS are the long metal arms which reach in between the uplifted warps in the weaving process in modern looms and pass the weft back and forth; a job performed earlier by the shuttle which carried a package of yarn rolled up in it, paying it out as it travelled. Rapier looms and water-jet looms have made the wooden shuttle largely redundant.

REED a type of comb which keeps the warp threads in order and beats up the weft threads during weaving.

RETTING is a process used with Flax and Hemp (both vegetable sources of fiber) not unlike fermentation, but where the unwanted material, gum, woody matter etc., softens, dissolves or separates from the long stem fibers which are to be retained and further processed. There is 'dew' retting, 'pond' retting, 'steam' retting and chemical retting.

ROVING OR SLUBBING a lightly twisted rope of fibers from which yarn is spun.

SAW GIN a type of cotton gin in which the fibers are pulled away from the seed by the action of rapidly revolving saws.

SHEDDING separating the warp threads in the weaving to form a passage way in the shape of a V so that the weft can be inserted.

SKEWER a long slender wooden rod for holding the roving bobbins on the top of a roving or spinning frame.

SLEY or GOING PART the frame which moves backwards and forwards to make picking and beating up easier during weaving.

SPOOL a word generally meaning a double headed bobbin but the words spool and bobbin are general terms and often interchangeable. In the UK and The States they have slightly different implications, though experts disagree on exactly what these are!

STAPLE a fiber of cotton, wool, flax and the like.

SHIELDS are the metal protective bands wrapping the top and bottom flanges.

TRASH unwanted bits of seed, leaf, twig etc. which need to be removed from the raw fiber.

TWIST, DIRECTION OF a yarn or cord has an 's' twist if, when held in a vertical position the spirals conform in slope to the central portion of the letter 's', and 'z' twist if the spirals conform in slope to the central portion of the letter 'z'.

TWISTING the process of combining two or more ends into a ply yarn or cord. Also refers to adding twist to a single yarn to obtain greater strength and smoothness, increased uniformity or to obtain novelty effects.

WARP the threads running lengthways in weaving, having extra tensile strength.

WEFT the threads in weaving which go across the fabric.

WINDER machines used for winding yarn into a package such as a cone or tube.

WORSTED a wide range of fabrics made from worsted yarns, generally constructed of smooth well twisted yarns. Typical examples are suiting fabrics, gabardine, serge, tropical worsted, dress fabrics, crepes etc. This interesting word derives from a small town called Worstead in Norfolk, England, from which cloth of an exceptional quality was made famous, probably in the 1600s.

Where the symbol ⬭ is shown, it means that a Dixon Driver is fitted under the bobbin (see page 54). It does not mean necessarily that the bobbin was made by Dixons of England although many of them were.

Measurements are given, first: overall height 'A', secondly: diameter of base 'B'. Sometimes, the diameter of the top 'C' will be given as a third dimension.

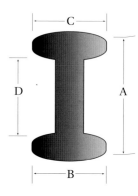

Measurements of bobbins in this book are given overall 'A'... as the man in the street would see them, but this is NOT STRICTLY CORRECT. A millworker would look at this particular bobbin ... and call it an EIGHT BY FOUR. This is because the 8" INSIDE measurement 'D', which determines its carrying capacity, is the critical one in the mill. Nevertheless we have stayed with the man-in-the-street dimensions stated since this book is written from a casual collectors standpoint. Now you have this piece of specialised information to impress with, here's another ... the dimension 'D' is called the 'LIFT' size. The bobbin above has an 8" lift.

Numbering method:

 This box denotes that the bobbin was located in England and so presumed English.

 This box denotes that the bobbin was located in America and so presumed American.

We have done our best to ensure that descriptions are accurate but there are difficulties: methods vary in the two different countries of origin. Also some bobbins are simply too old for living memory. Finally it is fair to say that conflicting information is abundantly available, and often from the most impressive sources!